RICHARD NIXON, WATERGATE, AND THE PRESS

A Historical Retrospective

Louis W. Liebovich

PRAEGER

Westport, Connecticut
London

Library of Congress Cataloging-in-Publication Data

Liebovich, Louis.
    Richard Nixon, Watergate, and the press: a historical retrospective/Louis W.
Liebovich.
        p. cm.
    Includes bibliographical references (p.) and index.
    ISBN 0–275–97915–6 (alk. paper)
    1. Nixon, Richard M. (Richard Milhous), 1913—Relations with journalists.
2. Nixon, Richard M. (Richard Milhous), 1913—Public opinion.   3. Watergate
Affair, 1972–1974—Press coverage.   4. Watergate Affair, 1972–1974—Public
opinion.   5. United States—Politics and government—1969–1974.   6. Press and
politics—United States—History—20th century.   7. Presidents—United States—
Biography.   8. Public opinion—United States.   I. Title.
E856.L54   2003
973.924′092—dc21
    [B]   2002029770

British Library Cataloguing in Publication Data is available.

Library of Congress Catalog Card Number: 2002029770
ISBN: 0–275–97915–6

First published in 2003

Praeger Publishers, 88 Post Road West, Westport, CT 06881
An imprint of Greenwood Publishing Group, Inc.
www.praeger.com

Printed in the United States of America

The paper used in this book complies with the
Permanent Paper Standard issued by the National
Information Standards Organization (Z39.48–1984).

10   9   8   7   6   5   4   3   2   1

This book is dedicated to my father, Albert Liebovich.

Contents

Prologue

Richard Nixon's inauguration in 1969 marked one of the strangest and most unexpected comebacks in political history and the turning point in America's tumultuous social rebirth. It accompanied a shift in political values and served as a prologue to the most tragic episode in American presidential politics. These obvious themes are yardsticks by which most scholars have measured the Nixon presidency.

Yet, a generation later, evidence points to trends that have carried beyond the dysfunctional 1970s. The Nixon legacy includes deteriorating press-president relations and the loss of public confidence in the Washington news-gathering process. Documenting that evolution will be the goal of this book as it examines the press structure of the Nixon White House, a prototype for modern White House–reporter antagonism. The break-in at the Watergate hotel and office complex launched a drama that deposed a president and changed American attitudes about government, but the break-in was only a minor manifestation of a long-range strategy outlined by a White House clique who never grasped their primary responsibilities and who approached their obligations with unparalleled vindictiveness. Watergate was ordained by marred White House logic, evident in the earliest Oval Office conversations and lasting until the president's farewell speech in 1974 on the White House lawn. It was not so much the nature of the underhanded malfeasance that led to the administration's destruction as it was the underlying convictions that justified them. As part of the White House's siege mentality, Nixon and his subordinates created a communications structure in January 1969 that signaled a changing press-president relationship and almost guaranteed a tragedy.

Indeed, what followed were wholesale violations by men who understood that they were breaking the law. We have been reminded repeatedly of the consequences: imprisonment of some of the nation's most powerful leaders, a diminished presidency, shared embarrassment, public cynicism, lost government initiatives, and eventual voter indifference. As those memories fade into the twenty-first century, however, one legacy may survive: implacable press relations and shallow reporting. Washington journalism changed after Watergate. From Gerald Ford to Bill Clinton, the quality of news and the interrelationship between the White House and the press corps steadily diminished.

How did the Watergate mentality develop? What led to the illegal acts and to the paranoia that propelled those deeds? Who planned the public denigration of reporters and the spying? Who developed the policies that would alienate reporters for the sixty-seven months of the Nixon presidency and for years to come? How did the Nixon press apparatus differ from previous presidencies', and was it a model for the ones that followed? What does this mean to the presidency a generation after Nixon's resignation? Did the press corps need to be curbed, and were the administration's actions understandable, if not condonable, as a defense against a wholly unfair group of correspondents? Why does Watergate still reverberate in the twenty-first century? These questions will be addressed, as we stir the ashes thirty years later. This book will explore not so much the events but the strategy, especially as it related to the news media.

The catalyst for this book was my conversation with a radio talk show host in 1999 during President Bill Clinton's impeachment hearings. Were the causes of the Nixon resignation and the Clinton impeachment similar? he asked. Of course they were not, and I sensed that he felt obliged to ask on behalf of his audience, which probably had forgotten or had never known about Watergate. Few events in American history were more dramatic and more traumatic. Yet, a generation later, a majority of Americans either are ignorant of the details of Watergate or fail to understand the causes of the scandal and role the press played. They understand that something in Washington is amiss and that reporters do not cover the White House in the tradition of past years, but few comprehend why this is so. There are at least five reasons for this: (1) the natural forgetting process; (2) a tendency to omit from memory a tragedy that embarrassed and disgusted the entire country; (3) the complexity of Watergate; (4) the intricacies of White House press relations; and (5) obfuscation by the Nixon people.

No ex-presidential family has gone to such lengths to block access to files and historical documents as the Nixons have. A generation after Watergate and years after an agreement was reached to release thousands of hours of White House documents and taped conversations, scholars were still wrestling with the federal government and Nixon family lawyers for the right to allow the public to review those recordings and papers. The Nixons screened all the materials and then demanded $200 million in compensation from the government for papers and tapes seized by authorities when Nixon resigned in 1974. Nixon died in 1994. Finally, in 2000, in exchange for a government payment of $18 million, the Nixon family agreed to release the tapes and papers. Nearly all of them were to have been made public by 2003. Some interesting conversations were made public in the tapes released in 2002. In March of that year it was revealed that Nixon in 1971 had discussed with Henry Kissinger, his foreign affairs advisor, the possibility of using nuclear weapons in Vietnam. It was a passing remark in a lengthy conversation, but it chilled even the most ardent Nixon supporters. In a tape also released in March 2002, it was revealed that Nixon and Billy Graham, a popular evangelist minister, had both expressed their disgust with liberal Jews. Graham said in 2002 that he did not remember making the remark but apologized anyway.

Nixon had tried to keep that kind of exchange private. Until the tapes were released, little of that kind of exchange became public. Documents released to the public at the National Archives II in College Park, Maryland, are suspiciously bereft of damning personal comments and exchanges. The Presidential Materials Review Board, for reasons other than national security, has removed thousands of texts from files, and many thousands of files have never even been considered for public scrutiny because of legal restraints put in place by the Nixon family. For instance, in Press Secretary Ronald Ziegler's papers, a documents withdrawal notice placed in a folder advises that all documents from August 2, 1973, to the end of the file (during the height of the Watergate investigation) had been removed from public scrutiny at Nixon's behest because "the contents of this [entire] folder are objectionable."[1] In another example, a Presidential Materials Review Board certificate in a folder in Chief of Staff H. R. Haldeman's papers has been inserted as a replacement for most of Haldeman's notes from February 7, 1973, to March 31, 1973, during the Watergate cover-up. The certificate declares that public release of twenty-three documents was contested by Haldeman, and so the board decided to remove all but six pages from public access—three for national security reasons, eleven for invasion of privacy justifications, and three for both invasion of privacy and national security justifications. No supporting explanation as to why the documents were removed was offered, so the public will never know Haldeman's thinking and planning during those crucial days.[2] His widow published Haldeman's daily notations from his four years in the White House in 1993, but even that material actually represents only "a balanced condensation" of Haldeman's memos.[3] A match with the original daily ledger at National Archives II indicates some fairly selective judgment on the part of the Haldeman family.

The Nixons were paid $18 million in exchange for documents, files, and tapes seized by the government after the president resigned. For a generation the dispute prevented the release of thousands of documents and more than 3,000 hours of taped conversations. Finally, through the efforts of a University of Wisconsin legal scholar, Stanley I. Kutler, copies of the 201 hours of Abuse of Power and Cabinet Room tapes were released in 1996 and then were put on sale to the public in January 2000. The family finally settled for $18 million in June 2000, sending most of the money to the Nixon Presidential Library in Yorba Linda, California.

Meanwhile, Watergate participants, including journalists who covered Washington, have never been reluctant to place their spin, pro or con, on historical events. Nearly everyone involved wrote a book about his experiences. Most of these works appeared in the 1970s, with many landing on the *New York Times* best-seller list. Beginning with the Nixon–David Frost series of television interviews in the spring of 1977, Nixon and many of his subordinates emerged from years of seclusion after the resignation to make controlled public appearances in hopes of convincing the public that Watergate was an overblown media contrivance. They argued that they had committed no acts that other presidents and their assistants had not effected before them. Then, after an orgy of Watergate admissions and explanations, Americans grew weary of the entire series of events and the forgetting process took hold, resulting in the Watergate amnesia of the early twenty-first century.

Another curious research phenomenon: historians seem to have collectively forfeited responsibility for evaluating this period to the participants. Some present-day historians even apologize for writing "another Watergate book." Noted presidential historian Joan Hoff-Wilson in 1992 studied approximately eight hundred articles and books written on Watergate by "elite social critics." Hoff-Wilson described the historical record of the Nixon presidency as "the worst single body of literature on any president that I have ever read."[4]

As thousands of hours of White House tapes and documents were apparently being readied for public scrutiny, there were those who argued that nothing new could be written on Watergate. Yet, the 201 hours of Abuse of Power and Cabinet Room tapes released in 1996 alone provide convincing proof that many of the books written in the 1970s, particularly by White House occupants, were filled with misleading statements and half-truths. More than 3,500 hours of tapes and tens of thousands of new documents were made available after 1996.[5] (By 2001, 102 hours of tapes had been withheld for national security reasons, and it was likely that more would be withheld.) Much of the record still requires clarification. Not only is another Watergate book needed, but also a whole genre of works is in order to set the record straight.

The press was clearly a Nixon obsession. Much has been written about the treatment of correspondents, but only recently have scholars analyzed what the conflict has meant to the presidency and to the public. This book assesses the strategy of the times and recounts the damage that resulted then and for years afterward. It is about the press and the Nixon administration, but it explores much more than the events of the early 1970s. It places the entire press-president relationship since that time into a historical retrospective.

NOTES

1. Press Secretary Ronald Ziegler Papers, "White House Information Officer's File," Box 13, August 2, 1973, National Archives II, College Park, Maryland (all subsequent archival documents are from National Archives II unless otherwise indicated).

2. Chief of Staff H. R. Haldeman's Papers, Box 47, diary notes from February 7 to March 31, 1973.

3. H. R. Haldeman, *The Haldeman Diaries: Inside the Nixon White House* (New York: G. P. Putnam's Sons, 1994), xiii.

4. Joan Hoff-Wilson, "discussant" in Leon Friedman and William F. Levantrosser, eds., *Watergate and Afterward: The Legacy of Richard M. Nixon* (Westport, Conn.: Greenwood, 1992), 263.

5. Archival information provided to the author April 19, 1999, updated in November 1999 and again in December 2000.

Acknowledgments

A special note of appreciation is extended to Yuanzhi Zhou, David Bruser, Elena Ferrarin, and Kelly Coleman, my research assistants, whose perseverance at the microfilm machines enhanced this study immeasurably.

Chapter 1

The Missing Honeymoon

From the earliest days of the new administration, it was clear that there would be no peace between the staff of President Richard Nixon and the Washington-based news media. Press Secretary Ronald Ziegler claimed later that press relations were normal, even cordial, in those first few months in 1969, but it is obvious that no other president had entered the White House determined to go to war immediately with the news media and correspondents. If relations were normal, they were so only on the surface, and even that tentative congeniality would be gone by November 1969. Every previous American chief executive who took office in the twentieth century found that handling the press was a most difficult task, but each at first attempted to pacify the journalists, whose words could greatly affect public perceptions. Even Herbert Hoover and Dwight D. Eisenhower, who regarded reporters as nuisances, proffered conciliatory gestures and some modest concessions upon taking office. Usually, this was at the behest of the press secretary, who himself had been a reporter and who understood that news flow was a two-way street where the president had to provide information and answers in order to promote programs and ideas.

Fluctuations in the relationship between correspondents and White House staff started before Nixon took office. During the Lyndon Johnson administration of 1963–1969, a change of press secretary every year and the dissemination of deceptive information about the Vietnam War strained relations, altering the correspondents' perceptions of the press office and the White House. Unlike Nixon, though, Johnson spoke frequently with reporters. The problems resulted not necessarily from truculence or silence, but from Johnson's heavy-handed tactics and overbearing manner. This, coupled with reporters' negative stories about Vietnam, brought friction and mutual mistrust, but a modicum of civility still existed.

As Johnson's term was ending, however, events in the spring of 1968 during the primary election campaign horrified and disillusioned journalists and the public alike. After the assassinations of Martin Luther King, Jr., and Robert F. Kennedy, voters lost enthusiasm for the electoral process. The tone of reporting about national politics turned decidedly negative. The bloody street confrontations in Chicago during the summer Democratic National Convention only reinforced that malaise. By the end of the tumultuous year, tension existed between reporters and the White House, and the public distrusted both. Nixon had carefully revived his nearly dead career after losing a presidential campaign to John F. Kennedy by 118,000 votes in 1960 and a California gubernatorial bid to Pat Brown in 1962. Nixon's cleverness in taking advantage of such calamitous political events to win the White House was one of the amazing stories of the modern electoral process. But press-president relations had already begun to deteriorate before Nixon took office, and the job he faced, after such a violent and chaotic year, would have given pause to any person in late 1968.

To Nixon's credit, he recognized the mood of the country and on election night offered the country encouragement. After concession speeches by Hubert Humphrey and George Wallace, the president-elect recalled a teenager's placard during a campaign stop in Deshler, Ohio. The sign read, "Bring Us Together." Nixon told a cheering audience: "And that will be the great objective of this administration at the outset, to bring the American people together."[1] Ironically, what Nixon and his people accomplished was the exact opposite. In sum, that promise and its hollowness prolonged a long period of disillusionment for the American electorate. It also made permanent the decline in relations between the press and the president.

But in late 1968 Nixon was the conquering hero and the country hoped to put the rancor behind. Few would have predicted that Nixon's terms in office would be as antagonistic to the press and as disconcerting as the Johnson administration's. As president-elect, Nixon moved quickly with his agenda, while screening reporters out of the information loop. On December 11, 1968, Nixon used a television address, not a press conference, to announce his entire list of cabinet officers, an unusual move and one meticulously designed to undercut press speculation and short-circuit the print media's hunger for preinauguration stories. It was a clear signal to reporters what lay ahead. This was reinforced days later when Nixon called the Cabinet designees and their wives together in the White House and told them:

Always remember, the men and women of the news media approach this as an adversary relationship. The time will come when they will run lies about you, when the columnists and editorial writers will make you seem to be scoundrels or fools or both and the cartoonists will depict you as ogres. ... Now don't let this get you down—don't let it defeat you. ... This is part of the process of communicating with the country and part of your job.[2]

That advice captured the essence of Nixon's approach to press relations. He had built a meteoric career by manipulating reporters, but his bitter defeats in

1960 and 1962 convinced him that it was not his personal shortcomings but a "liberal press" that had stymied his career. This theme accompanied his every move in early 1969.

SPLIT PRESS RESPONSIBILITIES

Much has been made of Nixon's decision to split White House responsibility for publicity and press relations, but most observers miss the key point. It was Nixon and Chief of Staff H. R. Haldeman who planned and executed press strategy. The other staff members mattered little until 1973, when Haldeman was forced to resign. Puppets do not matter; the puppeteer does. Nixon received a sixty- to eighty-page daily news summary from aide Patrick Buchanan listing recent news focuses and taking note of attitudes toward Nixon. Nixon would then direct Haldeman to ask for press action or request that a member of the administration make adjustments or change course.[3] This structure denigrated the office of the press secretary and somewhat exonerates the culpability of the press secretary and the communications director, who were kept out of the loop. Nixon had named Herbert Klein as director of communications, instructing that Klein be responsible for promoting programs and ideas to Congress and the country. Ronald Ziegler served as press secretary, nominally working with White House correspondents by tending to their day-to-day technical needs, personally briefing them on daily activities in the White House, and deluging them with press releases. Klein, who had resigned as editor of the *San Diego Union* to join Nixon in the White House, had known Nixon and supported him for over twenty years. In the late 1960s the *Union* was one of the few remaining extremely conservative newspapers that encouraged bias among its editors and reporters and staunchly took sides in its news coverage and editorial policies. Klein may have been a journalist, but he was hardly the kind of standard, objective journalist of the post–World War II era. It is one of the ironies of the Nixon White House—the source of untold numbers of complaints about bias in the press—that the communications director had been one of the most blatantly partial journalists of his time. Ziegler, only twenty-nine at the time of his press assignment, had no journalistic experience, having been a tour guide at Disneyland and then an account executive working under Haldeman with the J. Walter Thompson advertising agency in the Los Angeles area.

It was Nixon's intention to manipulate and attack, not to inform or to establish a mutually respectful give and take. Yet, in reality, it was neither the Ziegler nor the Klein appointment that underscored this war mentality. It was the naming of Haldeman, the quintessential hatchet man, as chief of staff. A review of Haldeman's files shows that he controlled press relations and communications strategy while taking his direction daily from the president. Nixon and Haldeman met in the Oval Office each morning and discussed strategy, including how to best frustrate reporters and to promote Nixon's image. Haldeman then sent a fusillade of memos to Ziegler and Klein ordering them to follow certain approaches and demanding reports on their progress, always dropping veiled threats as to what would happen if deadlines were not met. Haldeman directed the taunts and the tactics against reporters, and he planned every detail of the vendetta. Nixon and Haldeman had little respect for either Ziegler or Klein. According to Haldeman's daily notes, Nixon as early as May 1969 described Ziegler as "a superb mechanic, but not a designer."[4] He added in the same diary entry: "Real problem, as he [Nixon] says, is that we don't have a real PR operator, at a very high level, who really works at this all day, every day. (Herb) Klein and (Bud) Wilkinson [Klein's assistant] are both very inadequate, and not *in* enough [Haldeman italics]."[5] That Ziegler was twenty-nine and that Klein was one of the least objective journalists in the country was actually immaterial, because both took their marching orders from the chief of staff anyway. Still, their lack of rapport with White House correspondents symbolically represented the gulf between the administration and the press, but their lack of access to Nixon's inner circle kept them from being enmeshed in the Watergate scandal.

This White House infrastructure left Haldeman with enormous strength, which he wielded unwaveringly until his forced resignation in April 1973 when Watergate gripped the White House. His staff memos dictated a range of press activities from the ridiculously minute to the sweeping reformulation of overall press strategy. Seven weeks after Nixon took office, Haldeman wrote in a memo to Klein, "Nixon wants the P living quarters to be referred to as the 'residence' rather than the Mansion, all staff to be notified."[6] A year later another memo provided an all-compassing directive about Nixon hatred and suspicion of the press:

(You are to get out) and run somewhere (the story) about how the President has overcome the great handicaps under which he came into office—specifically the hostile press epitomized by the NEW YORK TIMES, WASHINGTON POST, TIME, NEWSWEEK [Haldeman capitalization], the hostile network commentators, the generally hostile Congress, etc. This is the whole pitch that we talked about some time ago. The story has not been gotten through.[7]

A memo presidential aide Charles Colson wrote to Haldeman in April 1971 stated that a Nixon interview on March 22 with Howard K. Smith, an American Broadcasting Company news commentator, had not drawn a large audience because it had been aired opposite a popular movie. Haldeman passed the memo on to Ziegler, directing that a Nixon interview never again be scheduled against popular entertainment.[8] Just weeks before it was apparent that Haldeman had lost his usefulness to Nixon and that the president would ask for his resignation in April 1973, Haldeman was still dictating every communications detail. When Henry Kissinger negotiated a final peace agreement on Vietnam, Haldeman choreographed Kissinger's arrival in Paris down to the secretary of state's body movements. "No waves, smiles, etc.," Haldeman wrote in his personal notes that were passed on to Kissinger. He added: "Don't look at cameras. Imperative not smile—day of mourning," referring to former President Lyndon Johnson's death that week.[9] At a public speech in February 1973, print reporters were seated in front of Nixon and between the president and the audience. Haldeman wrote to himself in his daily notes to make certain such arrangements were changed. "In next four years—never again have press in front of P [Nixon] ... writing press was right in front of P."[10]

As his resignation approached, Haldeman was also still formulating overall press policy. He wrote a memo to himself on January 28, 1973, noting that he needed to devise for Ziegler a press strategy, "not just P's [Nixon's] hunches,"[11] that would carry the administration through the second term. Two weeks later, in a talking paper prepared for domestic advisor John Ehrlichman about a Nixon trip to Chicago for the ceremonial opening of a sewer plant, Haldeman wrote: "The Chicago sewer trip didn't help us at all, because nobody was interested in it. ... During this coming week we need to work out a strategy on the (Watergate Committee Chair Senator Sam) Ervin deal, an overall schedule plan, an overall PR approach. ... We especially need a PR policy that delineates what we're trying to accomplish."[12]

THREE STRATEGIES

Nixon and Haldeman pursued three press strategies: (1) influence the electorate directly by using television; (2) largely ignore the White House press corps (or flood it with inconsequential press releases) and spy on certain reporters whose negative stories had earned special White House enmity; and (3) verbally attack news institutions and reporters to keep them on the defensive. The televised announcement on his cabinet choices illustrates the first strategy. Nixon used televised addresses to the American public frequently in place of press conferences. Haldeman even bragged about this tactic in a parenthetical addendum to his published diary notes. He wrote that it was the Nixon White House strategy to schedule televised addresses rather than press conferences to ensure that all Nixon's words were carried directly to the public rather than have journalists summarize for the public the substance of a press conference. He added: "This tactic also made it possible for us to force coverage in prime time by scheduling the event at whatever time we wanted it to air. After a while, the networks got smart and quit providing simultaneous coverage on all three, but it was great while it lasted."[13]

There were many examples of Nixon attacks on and avoidance of the press during each stage of his presidency. In his entire presidential career, Nixon addressed only thirty-nine press conferences, far fewer than any of his immediate predecessors or successors, and many of those press conferences amounted to ugly confrontations marked by name calling.[14] At the same time, the Nixon staff moved the reporters from their usual haunts in the lobby, West Basement, and Roosevelt Room into a part of the basement where Kennedy had built his wading pool. The pool was cemented over and made into offices, allowing reporters more room but distancing most of them from the White House's everyday activities.

Then, just months after the inauguration in 1969, the White House hired Jack Caulfield, a New York City police detective, and Tony Ulasewicz, who had been working for the New York Bureau of Special Services, a special police investigative unit. Caulfield was on the White House payroll and worked in the Executive Office Building, but Ulasewicz was paid from private illegally collected funds. In the spring of 1969, columnist Joseph Kraft had displeased Nixon with negative written comments about Nixon's Vietnam War policies. Caulfield and another agent were ordered to plant a listening device in Kraft's Georgetown home. Kraft and his wife were in France, so the FBI was ordered to tap Kraft's hotel phone in Paris.[15] The illegal listening devices produced little information of value. Less than four months into the Nixon administration, the White House had crossed a line, and, significantly, the first target of illegal surveillance was a journalist.

That July, the secret White House detectives investigated details of Mary Jo Kopechne's death. Kopechne was killed when an automobile driven by Senator Edward Kennedy, a Democrat from Massachusetts and brother of the late President Kennedy, plunged into Massachusetts's Chappaquiddick Bay after a late-evening party. Nixon wanted firsthand all the dirt he could collect on his perceived political enemy, Senator Kennedy.

From 1969 to early 1971, the Nixon White House, with the help of Federal Bureau of Investigation Director J. Edgar Hoover and according to Nixon himself, placed wiretaps in the homes and offices of eighteen individuals—five newsmen and thirteen aides in the White House, State Department, and Defense Department. Nixon claimed in his memoirs that every president and attorney general did this in the post–World War II era. The Nixon wiretaps were placed to find out how sensitive security information was winding up on the front pages of newspapers, particularly the *New York Times*. Nixon's people learned nothing from the illegal surveillance.[16] Nixon does not mention either Ulasewicz or Caulfield in his memoirs, and he claimed incorrectly that all the wiretaps were legal.

Clearly, the surveillances had been set up by Haldeman and approved by Nixon. It is doubtful that either Ziegler or Klein was consulted or even informed. The real communications strategists, Nixon and Haldeman, had taken over early. All these tactics embodied the second of Nixon's strategies: to ignore or harass the White House press corps.

The personification of the third strategy came in the fall of 1969. Vice President Spiro Agnew assailed the television networks in speeches in Iowa and Alabama, accusing news executives of bias against Nixon. Haldeman aide Jeb Magruder spurred Nixon and Haldeman to step up the war against the media.

Magruder advised Haldeman in October 1969 that the White House should use a "rifle" of concentrated efforts against the media through personal attacks and pressure from the Federal Communications Commission, the antitrust division of the Attorney General's Office, and the Internal Revenue Service. The objective was to monitor and torment major media companies, particularly the *New York Times*, the *Washington Post*, and the three major networks.[17]

On November 3, 1969, three weeks after Magruder's memo, Nixon delivered a speech on Vietnam to a national television audience. Minutes after the address, television correspondents summarized and analyzed the president's words. This instant analysis upset Nixon, who wouldn't have minded except that the analysts commented that Nixon had nothing new to say. Nixon took great pride in his addresses and his speech-making abilities. Haldeman wrote in his diary memoirs that the entire White House staff often would spend the whole night after a Nixon speech calling around the country to persons important and not so important, monitoring their attitudes and reporting immediately to the president. Alexander Butterfield, an aide to the president, testified in court thirty years later that of the 50,000 letters and telegrams sent to the White House after the November 3 speech, probably 30,000 had been generated by calls from the White House to Nixon supporters.[18] At times, the staff had orders to convince legions of Nixon supporters to get "100 vicious dirty calls to the *New York Times* and *Washington Post* about their editorials (even though no idea what they would be)." Haldeman noted in an addendum to his diary, "The plea for 'vicious dirty calls' to the papers was to keep pressure on them from the public in the hope that they would consider the other viewpoint occasionally."[19] Nixon and Haldeman decided in November 1969 that it was time to act on Magruder's suggestions and expand this strategy.

During the 1968 campaign, Agnew, a former Maryland governor and Nixon's handpicked running mate, had repeatedly embarrassed Republicans with his misstatements and sweeping denunciations of segments of the public and press. Secretly, Nixon's people detested Agnew, were suspicious of his conservative support, and saw him as a mediocre politician with a pedestrian intellect. Haldeman was puzzled when Agnew hired one of Lyndon Johnson's former assistants and was convinced the man was a spy for the Democrats.[20] Agnew's worst gaffe during the campaign came when he referred to *Baltimore Sun* reporter Gene Oishi as a "fat Jap."[21] Agnew said later that Oishi was a friend and the remark was made in jest, but the thoughtless epithet came to be symbolic of Agnew's apparent lack of acumen and respect for ethnic inclusiveness. Haldeman and Nixon decided that it was Agnew who would lead the public war against the media. Already at odds with reporters and considered to be the most expendable person in the Nixon administration, Agnew appeared to be the perfect choice.

On November 13, 1969, in Des Moines, in a speech prepared by the White House, Agnew told a Republican audience that the television networks were operated by a "tiny and closed fraternity of privileged men, elected by no one, and enjoying a monopoly sanctioned and licensed by the government." Nixon had a right to communicate with the people without the media filtering his words, Agnew added.[22] The speech was carried live on all three networks, preempting scheduled programming. No one in high office had ever issued such a sweeping indictment of the national broadcast networks. Hubert Humphrey, Nixon's 1968 election opponent, who had remarked untold times about unfair treatment of him by network television during the campaign, hypocritically told reporters that Agnew had issued a "'calculated attack' on the right to dissent and on the media."[23]

AGNEW ATTACKS CONTINUE

During a speech in Montgomery, Alabama, the next week, Agnew expanded his assault to include the *Washington Post* and the *New York Times*, labeling both companies monopolies and renewing his call for "more voices" among the nation's press.[24] A few hours before Agnew took the podium, Ziegler was given a copy of a first draft of the speech. He wrote to Haldeman: "The Vice President has focused attention on a subject that has needed attention for a long time. ... I feel that, if the prime draft is delivered tonight as written, the Administration will be expanding its attack to our disadvantage." He advised that the speech be less provocative and added: "This latter approach, I fear, will force the media into a position which will [create] a gap in press relations between this Administration and the press that will be long-lasting in effect."[25] Haldeman and Nixon agreed and the speech, which had been written by speechwriter (and future presidential candidate) Patrick Buchanan, was toned down, but Haldeman conceded in his diary: "It still hits very hard, especially at the *New York Times*. I did get out the highly personal and defensive segments."[26]

The Agnew attacks raised a furor and called public attention to how networks and the nation's top newspapers and magazines covered Washington.

ABC President Leonard Goldenson's response to the Agnew attacks was typical of network reaction. Goldenson's statement said:

As I said last week, after the VP's first speech, I firmly believe that in our free society, the ultimate judges of the reliability of our news presentation will be the viewing public. Again, I leave it to the public, to determine whether the VP's renewed attack today, is an attempt to intimidate and discredit not only TV news reporting but other major news media. Personally, I believe it is. I hope we are not facing a period in the history of our nation when high government officials try to act both as judge and jury on the issue of a free press.[27]

Interestingly, it was James Hagerty, a vice president of ABC and formerly president Dwight D. Eisenhower's press secretary for eight years, who called in the statement. Frank Stanton, CBS president, called Agnew's remarks an "unprecedented attempt by the Vice President of the United States to intimidate a news medium which depends for its existence upon government licenses." NBC President Julian Goodman said that Agnew's "attack on television news is an appeal to prejudice."[28]

The propriety and fairness of network news coverage is necessarily and properly debated openly in a democratic society. No set of institutions, including the national news media, should operate under anything less than the most intense public scrutiny. It is clear that the national press corps and their home networks, newspapers, magazines, and wire services are a collection of competing groups and individuals, who are both human and fallible. As one of Ziegler's successors, Jody Powell (Jimmy Carter's press secretary) would note years later, the White House press corps had too often become a group of arrogant and self-serving individuals who wished to serve their egos more often than inform the public.

An incident involving Ziegler's office in April 1973 underscores this point. NBC and CBS White House correspondents Richard Valeriani and Robert Pierpoint wanted special parking privileges. Ziegler aide J. Bruce Whelihan sent the press secretary a memo informing him that Valeriani and Pierpoint were upset because ABC's Tom Jarriel had a special parking spot in the West Wing executive parking lot. Valeriani's and Pierpoint's spaces were located in the less prestigious Ellipse parking area. The West Wing spot had previously been used by former ABC correspondent Bill Lawrence, who had needed the more conveniently located spot because of health problems, Whelihan wrote to Ziegler. Jarriel simply took over the parking space when Lawrence stopped covering the White House. Whelihan suggested that, to keep peace, Jarriel's assigned spot be moved to the Ellipse parking area.[29] Obviously, these delicate negotiations had no bearing on world peace or the national economy, but this much-ado-about-nothing tiff demonstrates the pompousness with which all press secretaries are forced to deal.

The real problem had nothing to do with the quality of reporting in the White House, the ideology of the nation's media, or the haughtiness of the correspondents. As has been pointed out, this attack was part of a three-pronged strategy to undercut the role of the media in covering the White House and in presidential politics. All modern presidential staffs deal with personalities, bloated egos, negative imagery, and ideologically motivated criticism from the media. Franklin D. Roosevelt claimed that 88 percent of the nation's newspapers opposed him politically, an exaggerated claim. The Nixon White House tolerated no criticism. It acted as if no previous president had ever been excoriated by editorial writers and criticized by commentators and columnists or unfairly depicted by correspondents. Nixon's people reacted to every slight and sought retribution against those who did not fall in line. Nixon had no interest in balanced coverage. He wanted exclusively favorable treatment at all levels, and so the potential for intelligent debate on the topic was lost.

The vindictiveness of the White House obviated any proper give-and-take. Yes, the media were and are too powerful at times and too monopolized. Yes, reporters can be biased and focus too often on personalities. But none of this was relevant when the Nixon White House sought only to bully and to manipulate. This was the real tragedy of the Nixon years: the traditional contentious but respectful relations between White House and correspondents deteriorated to mutual dislike and disrespect, and the topic of how powerful the press had become could not be reasonably debated amidst the hateful rhetoric.

ENEMIES AND FRIENDS

Within eighteen months of Nixon's taking office, the White House staff had hired private investigators and used the FBI to spy on journalists. It had created an "enemies list," consisting of people who had spoken or written something considered by the staff as anti-Nixon or who had opposed Nixon in a campaign or on an issue. The list, whose existence was revealed on May 22, 1973, by White House counsel John Dean during Watergate testimony, contained the names of labor leaders, entertainers, political opponents, antiwar activists, and civil rights leaders—persons not firmly committed to Nixon's cause, who were powerful or famous enough to warrant concern. About one in ten persons on the list of 182 was a journalist or news executive. The list included entertainers Bill Cosby, Gregory Peck, Jane Fonda, Dick Gregory, Steve McQueen, Paul Newman, Tony Randall, and Barbra Streisand, and New York Jets quarterback Joe Namath. Listed journalists and news executives included Jim Bishop, Jim Deakin, Rowland Evans, Charles Goodell, Julian Goodman, Stuart Loory, John Osborne, James Reston, Carl Rowan, Jack Anderson, Marquis Childs, Lesley Gelb, Marvin Kalb, Joseph Kraft, Mary McCrory, Daniel Schorr, Sander Vanocur, and Tom Wicker.[30] Many people not on the list were disappointed that they were considered not important enough to be included. Others found the document a chilling reminder that their movements could be under surveillance and every utterance recorded and filed in some secret dossier. The enemies list will be discussed further in later chapters; the point here is that Nixon's staff kept complete scorecards on journalists' attitudes—both positive and negative.

Some scorecards included journalists whom the staff felt could be counted on to support Nixon or who could be influenced to support the president. In June 1969, one of Klein's aides compiled a list of seventy-five White House correspondents and their attitudes. Here are the names on the first page of the list, followed by Klein's penned comments: Alexander Holmes, MacNaught Newspapers, "very good"; Robert S. Allen, Publisher's Hall Syndicate, "conservative, fair to us"; Joseph Alsop, *Los Angeles Times*, "good on Vietnam, but fair on domestic"; Stewart Alsop, *Newsweek*, "pro ABM"; Charles Bartlett, Publisher's Hall Syndicate, "Democratic tier"; Jim Batten, Knight newspapers, "moderate"; Bruce Biossat, Newspaper Enterprises, "very fair"; Thomas Braden, Field Syndicate, "favorable"; David Broder, *Washington Post*, "very objective, a reporter's reporter"; William Buckley, *Washington Star*, "conservative"; John Chamberlain [no ID], "excellent"; Marquis Childs, United Features, "not too good"; Saville Davis, *Christian Science Monitor*, "good to fair, straight reporting"; James Deakin, *St. Louis Post-Dispatch*, "surprisingly good"; Lyle Denniston, *Washington Star*, "fair"; Ralph de Toledano, King Features, "excellent"; Robert Donovan, *Los Angeles Times*, "very fair"; William Edwards, *Chicago Tribune*, "excellent"; Evans and Novak, Publisher's Hall Syndicate, "bad"; Ernest Ferguson, *Baltimore Sun*, "fair"; and Max Frankel, *New York Times*, "unpredictable but usually fair." The list continues for three more pages. These were obviously the opinions of Klein and his staff, in many cases far different from those of Haldeman or Nixon. There was, in fact, disagreement even among Klein and his aides. Some comments were changed. Frankel, for instance, was originally labeled "poor."[31]

Klein's office also assembled a list of news executives from around the country who he thought either were in the Nixon camp or could be brought around. This tabulation resulted when, on January 3, 1970, Haldeman wrote to Klein: "The president would like a list of the top few and most influential publishers and editors around the country—perhaps 10 or 20 with whom, as we go into the election year, he should maintain a fairly constant level of contact via phone calls, letters, etc. Another list should be made covering the top television producers."[32] Six weeks later, Klein offered thirty-one names: Jerry Greene, of the *New York Daily News*; Frank Kuest, U.S. Information Agency White House correspondent; Carl DeBloom, editor of the *Columbus (Ohio) Dispatch*; Brady Black, editor of the *Cincinnati Enquirer*; Alan Emory, of the North American Newspaper Alliance and the *Watertown* (New York) *Times*; Peter Hacks, of NBC News; George Hermann, of CBS News; Paul Block, publisher of the *Toledo Blade*; Bill Moyers, publisher of *Newsday* (and previously one of Lyndon Johnson's press secretaries); James Cox, president of Cox Broadcasting; Gilbert P. Smith, president of the Associated Press Managing Editors Association; Joseph Benti, of CBS; John R. Cauley, of the *Kansas City Star*; Harold E. Clancy of the *Boston Herald Traveler*; J.A. Clendinen, of the *Tampa Times*; Emmett Dedmon, vice president of the *Chicago Sun-Times*; Willard Edwards and Clayton Kirkpatrick, of the *Chicago Tribune*; Richard Hollander, of the *Washington Daily Times*; Norman E. Isaacs, president of the American Society of Newspaper Editors; Jenkin Lloyd Jones, Sr., of the *Tulsa Tribune*; Ted Lewis, of the *New York Daily News*; Felix McKnight, of the *Dallas Times Herald*; August Meyer, president of WCIA Channel 3 in Champaign, Illinois; Alan L. Otten, of the *Wall Street Journal*; Victor Riesel, a columnist with Publisher's Hall Syndicate; Sol Taishoff, owner of several broadcasting industry publications; Frank VanDerLinden, a news executive with newspapers in Greenville, S.C., Jackson, Miss., and Nashville, Tenn.; John C.A. Watkins, of the *Providence Journal & Bulletin*; and W.D. Workman, Jr., of *The State* in Columbia, S.C. Gerhard D. Bleicken, an officer of the John Hancock Mutual Life Insurance Company, was also on the list, but it is unclear why Klein would list an insurance company executive among a dossier of friendly news executives.[33]

Klein was assigned to badger anyone who was expected to support Nixon but seemed to waver. Klein wrote to Otis Chandler, publisher of the *Los Angeles*

Times, on July 16, 1970, to complain about a column by Stuart Loory in which Loory questioned the effectiveness of Henry Kissinger, special presidential advisor on foreign affairs.[34] Chandler brushed off Klein's inquiry a month later, saying in a note that Kissinger had authenticated the information that was in the column and that he (Chandler) did not control a columnist's opinion, at any rate.[35] Klein did not let the issue drop, however. Under the Chandler family leadership, the *Times* had supported Nixon from the beginning of his career, and it was apparently inconceivable to White House staffers that the most powerful newspaper in California could not be brought to heel. Klein and Chandler met in Los Angeles in August and had a frank and "productive" talk. "I told him that in many ways the *L.A. Times* had the option to become the hometown newspaper of the White House, particularly with the attitude of the *New York Times* and the *Washington Post*," Klein wrote to Haldeman.[36] Obviously, Klein thought he held more sway with Chandler than he did, because *Los Angeles Times* coverage of the Nixon White House became more critical as months passed. In fact, by January 1971 Loory was writing about the cost to taxpayers of the Nixon Western White House in San Clemente and Nixon was demanding of his staff that Loory be banned from the White House.[37]

Klein's, Haldeman's, and Ziegler's offices monitored reports on the broadcast and print media. Haldeman often demanded that action be taken in response to any negative report about the White House. In October 1969 Haldeman asked Klein to do something about an unfavorable segment of an NBC newscast detailing protests against the war in Vietnam and military conscription. Klein wrote to Haldeman, "I have discussed NBC's September 20 news program with Reuven Frank [of NBC News] who agreed to review the newscast. ... Second, I have asked our people in New York, Chicago, and Washington to generate letters to NBC criticizing the coverage that evening." In April 1970, Haldeman wrote to Klein, "It is obvious that the networks are running about twice a week five-minute series of interviews with unemployed people—the purpose apparently being to try to establish a recession psychology. Is there anything we can do to combat this effort?"[38]

Sometimes, the monitoring reached the ludicrous stage. Nixon's opponents picked up on a derogatory characterization left over from early congressional campaigns when his detractors referred to him as "Tricky Dick." On November 5, 1973, Don Meredith, the ever-sarcastic and irreverent color commentator for ABC's *Monday Night Football*, referred to Nixon on the air as Tricky Dick. A series of memos subsequently bounced around the White House. Jerry Warren, one of Ziegler's aides, wrote to the press secretary: "Gene Cowan called this afternoon to say the ABC executives here are appalled by Don Meredith calling the President 'Tricky Dick' during last Monday night's ABC football game. Gene said Meredith will open the show tonight at 9:00 p.m. by apologizing to the president."

No newspaper was too small or insignificant, if it carried anti-Nixon comments. The Nixon reelection committee considered a lawsuit against the *Hudson Dispatch* of Jersey, City, New Jersey, in November 1972, when the newspaper carried a paid advertisement by the local Democratic Party calling Nixon "Tricky Dick." White House lawyers advised the reelection committee to complain to the Office of Federal Elections.[39] Nixon staffers even huffed and puffed about Nixon's not being named Man of the Year by *Time* magazine in 1970.[40]

PRESS COVERAGE HISTORICALLY

Presidents and reporters are naturally at odds. Antagonism tends to rise in times of controversy, and certainly no period in American history lapsed into public dispute more than the Vietnam War era. The fall of 1969 was the height of antiwar unrest; some college campuses approached academic gridlock because of student demonstrations. Nixon would have been at odds with both reporters and segments of the public no matter what approach his staff had taken.

Certainly, the public had tired of the Vietnam War by 1969. The Tet Offensive, a failed military initiative by the Vietcong and North Vietnamese regulars in January 1968, had changed public opinion drastically (the attack looked successful on television) and convinced Johnson not to seek another term. Even so, the public was used to supporting the president, especially during wartime, and Nixon had a great advantage in 1969. He referred to the preponderance of the public, who supported his policies, as the "Silent Majority." In fact, it was neither silent nor a majority. Nixon had won by a minority vote in the 1968 election, and he personally was not popular among the general public. However, the presidency still held respect and admiration among the World War II generation, who had revered Franklin D. Roosevelt and respected Harry Truman, Dwight Eisenhower, and John F. Kennedy. Not even the Vietnam conflict changed the romance between the public and the presidency, and most Americans wished the newly elected Nixon success and hoped for an honorable end to the conflict in Asia, if any such goal could be reached.

As to the media, the public had had its doubts for years. Television had particularly become worrisome to the person on the street by 1969. Vance Packard's best-selling book, *The Hidden Persuaders*, published in 1957, suggested that advertisers could play with unwary viewers' minds without their realizing what was happening. The quiz show scandals of the late 1950s had reinforced the suspicion that television was largely a hoax on the public. Southern whites in the 1950s and early 1960s resented the depiction of police and white citizens in the South as bigots who met civil rights demonstrators with brute force (even though that is an accurate reflection of many confrontations) and grumbled about the Northern, liberal press.

The Agnew attacks of November 1969, then, drew much public sympathy, not just among conservatives but among a majority of Americans, who had tired of the war but who still wanted an honorable settlement to the conflict and who resented the "effete, impudent snobs," as Agnew labeled antiwar activists. These readers and viewers eagerly accepted the thesis that the networks and national print news media were in league with the long-haired protesters. The White House strategy of setting off the network newscasters and major print media correspondents as evil-minded manipulators was a clever one.

Few Americans sympathized with either protesters or journalists, and many wanted to believe that an exploitative press corps was duping them. Something sinister had to be behind all the turmoil and changing values of the 1960s. It had to be a few agitators and the ambitious and immoral news establishment. Nixon's suspicion of the New Left, anti-war liberals who opposed the "establishment," including traditional liberals, and the news media found a sympathetic audience in late 1969, and Agnew's attacks tapped into a vein of resentment. By the end of 1969, Agnew was the third most admired person in the country, behind the Rev. Billy Graham and Nixon. As a veteran of World War II, when patriotism had swept the country and touched nearly every American, Nixon shared a certain bond with the generation that controlled the country in the late 1960s and early 1970s. The dislike and disrespect for the antiwar movement was genuine on Nixon's part, and it was matched by the preponderance of the voting public. The obfuscation came in Nixon's ability to tie the antiwar movement and the news media together. As events would show later, the public's support of Nixon's war tactics and his denigration of the press were both misplaced.

The White House strategy was dangerous to the political health of both Nixon and the Republican Party, especially because the principals involved in the scheming had spied on reporters and illegally wiretapped their homes and offices. A percentage of the public may have adored Nixon and Agnew in 1969, but that was only because the attacks on the media, especially the networks, had cast the White House as victims of a bullying media establishment. Should the truth about the wiretaps and other Nixon White House dirty tricks become public, the image would switch, and that is the risk Nixon strategists faced after Agnew's speeches in 1969.

The Agnew attacks also brought into the open the antagonism that had been building from the time Nixon had been elected. Roosevelt had complained bitterly that the nation's newspapers favored Republican ideology and goals, but FDR and all other presidents before Nixon had usually kept their denunciations in house or had generalized their charges enough to assail the media as a whole without making the disagreement personal. The Nixon strategy was personal. Agnew referred to an elite handful of news executives. It didn't take long for the public to identify those persons. They saw the anchors and White House reporters every night during newscasts, and top network news executives were forced to respond in written statements. Agnew's remarks had drawn the public into this dogfight and had indirectly named the dogs. This signaled to reporters that times had permanently changed in the White House. They could expect no consideration or any cooperation. Criticism of the Nixon administration would meet with hostility from both the public and the White House and affect their lives and jobs. Yet, if they backed off and protected themselves, they knew they could be compromising the entire role of the media in Washington. This rock-and-a-hard-place juxtaposition caused discomfort and stress for journalists who had plenty of both anyway. Most reporters matched the White House's hard-line approach, and so four years of skirmishing followed.

TROUBLED 1960S END

As Nixon's first year in office came to an end so did the 1960s. The first twelve months had been modestly successful domestically for Nixon, but the dominating issue was still the war in Southeast Asia and no resolution to that conflict seemed in sight. In March of 1968 a U.S. Army platoon had slaughtered the inhabitants of a remote village in South Vietnam. The My Lai massacre became emblematic of what antiwar activists saw as the quintessential dilemma of Vietnam. American policy seemed to be directed toward saving the Vietnamese by destroying them. The massacre became public in the summer of 1969. During his court-martial in 1971, the leader of the platoon, Lt. William Calley, told the court that Vietcong were suspected to be in the village. None of the soldiers could distinguish between nonuniformed Vietcong and innocent civilians, so the entire village was wiped out. Calley was sentenced to life in prison at hard labor, but Nixon commuted his sentence to twenty years and eventually freed him. The story dominated the headlines off and on in 1969 and again in 1971, disillusioning even the World War II generation. Nixon made overtures to North Vietnamese leaders in Hanoi about peace talks in the spring of 1969. Johnson had authorized talks, but the negotiations never advanced past haggling over the shape of the table. Kissinger began secret talks on August 4, 1969, in Paris. Those negotiations would last three years, as the fighting continued. Meanwhile, protests on U.S. campuses increased in intensity, and leaders called for a Moratorium Day on October 15, asking students to boycott classes. The moratorium reminded Americans that the war was not near an end. Nixon began to fear that the poison that drove Johnson from office might send him packing, too. Nixon knew the war had to end, but he knew, too, that he could not appear to abandon the soldiers who fought in Southeast Asia. No one in the White House could publicly acknowledge that the war was lost. The public had to be eased into accepting that fact.

Perhaps Nixon's most ignominious defeat in his early months in office came late in 1969 when Clement F. Haynsworth, his nominee to replace the retiring Abe Fortas on the U.S. Supreme Court, was rejected by the Senate, fifty-five to forty-five with seventeen Republicans joining many of the Democrats. Haynsworth, of South Carolina, had a terrible record on civil rights. His nomination came ten years too late. No one with his record would be admitted to the high court after the activist 1960s. G. Harrold Carswell, of the Fifth Circuit Court of Appeals in Florida, also faced stiff opposition because of his segregationist voting record as a legislator in Georgia. He was rejected in April 1970 by a vote of 51 to 45. A month later, Harry Blackmun of Minnesota was confirmed. Two nominees had been rejected for one seat, a galling defeat for Nixon.

Not since the Kennedy administration had substantive talks taken place between the United States and the Soviet Union on arms controls. Soviet Ambassador to the United States Anatoly Dobrynin told Nixon in February 1969 that the Soviet Union was interested in beginning negotiations on arms limitations. Kissinger and Dobrynin met privately in the White House every week.[41] Also in February, Nixon visited Europe to discuss world security with leaders there. Nixon's strength lay in foreign policy because of his experience as a well-traveled vice president under Dwight D. Eisenhower, but his presidency received a boost on the domestic front when on July 20, 1969, Neil Armstrong became the first man to walk on the moon, enhancing U.S. prestige and brightening the public image of the Nixon administration.

The social service net that Johnson created with his Great Society programs was left intact by the Nixon administration, much to the surprise and disappointment of conservatives. In fact, Nixon expanded welfare to include the working poor in hopes of encouraging them to apply for jobs. The pundits began to refer to the quintessential Cold Warrior as a "moderate," though it was clear that "moderate" referred to a domestic agenda.

Meanwhile, inside the White House, Haldeman's tight grip on all matters large and small began to take its toll on the chief of staff. It was clear that Nixon and Haldeman needed a third person to share ultimate staff responsibilities and to monitor the details. John Ehrlichman's role as presidential advisor expanded as the year progressed. By the end of 1969 Ehrlichman, as special presidential assistant for domestic affairs, had attained the de facto role of co-chief of staff. For the next three-and-one-half years, Nixon, Haldeman, and Ehrlichman would direct every decision emanating from the White House with an ever-increasing emphasis upon manipulating or undercutting the press.

Yet, as the first year of Nixon's reign ended, the damage was still reversible. Few knew of the improprieties of the White House staff. Agnew's verbal attacks against the networks could have been dismissed as political gamesmanship. Certainly, Nixon had not damaged his image with the public. He was, after all, the same Nixon who, as an ambitious California congressman, had pursued Alger Hiss, a former assistant to the secretary of state, from the summer of 1948 to January 1950, when Hiss was convicted of perjury and sentenced to five years in prison. Hiss had been an acquaintance of Whittaker Chambers, an editor at *Time* magazine. Chambers was a reformed communist and insisted that Hiss had been a fellow party member while serving as an assistant in the State Department. That argument was never proven, because the statute of limitations on espionage charges had expired by the time the House Un-American Activities Committee, on which Nixon served, had begun to look into Hiss's background. It took a hung jury in one trial and a second trial before Hiss was convicted of perjury. Nixon had made a name for himself, and the national press had helped.

In 1952 at the outset of the general election campaign, Nixon, now a senator and vice presidential candidate, had come dangerously close to being dropped from the Republican ticket by Dwight D. Eisenhower because of revelations about an $18,000 political slush fund. During a lengthy paid address on national television, Nixon said he had never taken anything except a little dog named Checkers. He was going to keep the dog because his daughters loved it, he told his audience, without ever really addressing the question of the slush fund. The "Checkers Speech" worked and Nixon remained on the ticket, having cleverly used television to revive his career.

Nixon was a survivor, and controversy during the first year of his administration surprised neither the White House nor correspondents. Though Agnew had exposed media executives to public scorn, had the Nixon staff stepped back from what was happening and decided to take a different course in 1970, Nixon might have thrived as president with the press issue more or less forgotten. Nixon's expertise in international affairs particularly qualified him for the chief executive's office, and his experience in Washington suggested that he could handle Congress and the federal bureaucracy at least as effectively as Johnson, Kennedy, or Eisenhower. There was no question on either side of the press-president relationship, however, that the White House would not only continue its war on the Fourth Estate, but also would escalate it. The public's approbation of Agnew's tauntings seemed to reassure Nixon's people that he was supported by a silent majority that was not as vocal nor as visible as antiwar activists and journalists. Nixon strategists were convinced that this silent majority would side with the White House as the war with the press continued. Most of the country did not understand the implications of this manipulation. If there was anger and resentment among the general public toward the national news media, it was because of frustration with and fear of social change and a protracted war in Southeast Asia in the 1960s, but in such a volatile situation it took only a clever manipulator to tie that frustration and the press into a neat bundle. Haldeman had been searching for a method at the end of 1969, and Magruder's "rifle" memo struck a response. The Agnew fusillade signaled that the White House had concluded that more, not less, pressure needed to be applied to the press and that readers, viewers, and listeners were committed to a tough White House stance toward the nation's news media. This mentality would lead the president and his staff to a disdain for both the political process and the traditional role of the Fourth Estate. Bolstered by growing smugness, inch by inch they moved toward the abyss as they prepared for midterm elections and Nixon's own reelection campaign. With only sycophants permitted in the Nixon inner circle, no one spoke against this unhealthy course. The president and his staff were prisoners to both a paranoid ideology and a cloistered existence. The end of 1969 and the decision to take the White House's fear and loathing of the press to the public determined the fate of the Nixon presidency. In many ways, Watergate began in 1969. By 1972 and the actual break-in, the White House was so mired in a destructive mindset that a Watergate-type calamity was inevitable.

NOTES

1. Richard Nixon, *The Memoirs of Richard Nixon* (New York: Grosset & Dunlap, 1978), 335.

2. James Keogh, *President Nixon and the Press* (New York: Funk and Wagnalls, 1972), 2.

3. Stanley I. Kutler, *The Wars of Watergate* (New York: Knopf, 1990), 85.

4. H.R. Haldeman, *The Haldeman Diaries: Inside the Nixon White House* (New York: G.P. Putnam's Sons, 1994), entry of May 18, 1969, 58.

5. Ibid.

6. Communications Director Herbert Klein's Papers, Box 1, H.R. Haldeman to Herbert Klein memo, March 13, 1969.

7. Haldeman to Klein memo, Klein Papers, Box 1, February 4, 1970.

8. Press Secretary Ronald Ziegler's files, Box 18, Colson to HRH memo, April 19, 1971.

9. Haldeman Papers, Box 47, notes of January 23, 1973.

10. Haldeman Papers, Box 47, February 5, 1973 daily memo.

11. Haldeman Papers, Box 47, HRH daily memo, January 28, 1973.

12. Haldeman Papers, Box 47, Talking Paper to John Ehrlichman, February 10, 1973.

13. Haldeman, *The Haldeman Diaries*, June 16, 1969 entry, 64.

14. For complete texts of all of Nixon's press conferences see George W. Johnson, ed., *The Nixon Presidential Press Conferences* (New York: Earl M. Coleman Enterprises, 1978).

15. Joseph C. Spear, *Presidents and the Press: The Nixon Legacy* (Cambridge, Mass.: MIT Press, 1984), 133–34.

16. Nixon, *The Memoirs of Richard Nixon*, 389–90.

17. Daniel Schorr, *Clearing the Air* (Boston: Houghton-Mifflin, 1977), 39.

18. Associated Press wire story, June 13, 2000.

19. Haldeman, *The Haldeman Diaries*, November 3, 1969, entry, 104–05.

20. Ibid., 27.

21. Nixon, *The Memoirs of Richard Nixon*, 320.

22. Schorr, *Clearing the Air*, 39.

23. Ziegler Papers, Box 1, Speeches, Agnew Address to the Montgomery Chamber of Commerce, November 20, 1969.

24. Ibid.

25. Ziegler Papers, Agnew Speech file, Box 1, Ziegler to HRH memo, November 20, 1969.

26. Haldeman, *The Haldeman Diaries*, entry of November 20, 1969, 109.

27. "ABC Statement of Nov. 20, 1969, called in by James Hagerty," Ziegeler Papers, Box 1, Statements and Briefings.

28. Nixon, *The Memoirs of Richard Nixon*, 412.

29. J. Bruce Whelihan to Ziegler, memo, April 16, 1973, Ziegler Papers, Box 1, "Reorganization of the Press Office" file, 1–2.

30. "Positively Confidential/Eyes Only" memo from aide Diane Sawyer to Ronald Ziegler, Ziegler Papers, Box 1, memo file, 1–4.

31. "Journalist's [sic] Attitudes Toward the Nixon Administration," "Susie" to Klein memo, June 3, 1969, Klein Papers, Box 1, Haldeman Correspondence.

32. Haldeman to Klein, memo, January 3, 1970, Klein Papers, Box 1, Haldeman Correspondence.

33. Klein to Haldeman, memo, February 13, 1970, Klein Papers, Box 1.

34. Klein to Chandler, letter with a copy to Haldeman, July 16, 1970, Klein Papers, Box 1, Haldeman Correspondence.

35. Chandler to Klein, letter with a copy to Haldeman, August 12, 1970, Klein Papers, Box 1, Haldeman Correspondence.

36. Klein to Haldeman, confidential memo, September 1, 1970, Klein Papers, Box 1, Haldeman Correspondence.

37. Haldeman, *The Haldeman Diaries*, January 15, 1971, 117.

38. Haldeman to Klein, memo, April 13, 1970, Klein Papers, Box 1, Haldeman Correspondence.

39. Jerry Warren, memo to Ziegler, November 12, 1973, and Glenn J. Sedam, Jr., memos to Clark MacGregor, November 2, 1972, Ziegler Papers, Correspondence, Box 1.

40. Haldeman, *The Haldeman Diaries*, 116.

41. Nixon, *The Memoirs of Richard Nixon*, 369.

Chapter 2

Media Confrontations

Both the Republican Party and the Nixon White House looked forward to the 1970 congressional elections with great anticipation. Though the war in Southeast Asia continued to claim victims daily, Nixon blamed the Democrats for the war. Middle Americans had grown weary of the daily antiwar protests, and opinion surveys indicated that voters from both parties believed that Nixon had taken significant strides toward an honorable settlement, though what that settlement might be was wholly unclear. Nixon's approval rating in the Gallup poll, 68 percent, was at its highest ever in November 1969.[1]

Nixon proposed in May and Congress adopted in December 1969 a lottery system for drafting men who had been classified 1A, or fit for military service. Mirroring a system established during World War II, the annual lottery allowed draft-eligible men to plan their futures. A number was drawn at random for each day of the year, 1 through 365 or 366, and each draft-eligible man (mostly nineteen-year-olds unless they had received draft deferments) was assigned the number that matched his birthdate. Lotteries were held in ensuing years for those who became eligible in those years. The lower the number the better the chance of being conscripted. A number 200 or higher could reasonably assure a young man that he did not have to worry about the draft. This did not please those who opposed the war entirely, but the majority of Americans regarded it as an equitable system and it stifled protest for a short time. Although the lottery soothed concerns about the unfairness of the draft, it still allowed middle- and upper-income men to avoid conscription easily by enrolling in college for four years and receiving automatic deferments.

In sum, however, the perpetuation of peace negotiations and the institution of the draft lottery sparked hope that the war was at last being managed properly, a general feeling that had been lost to most Americans during the final years of the Johnson administration. It was merely a perception, but this war was mostly about perceptions anyway and GOP strategists hoped the relative calm over the war would lead to a sweeping Republican victory in the fall. Republicans had been the loyal opposition for forty years, with only brief tenures as the majority in either house of Congress. In the 1968 election Americans had voted in five additional Republicans in the Senate and four more in the House, but still the GOP trailed the Democrats, 58 to 42 and 243 to 192. By 1969, the Nixon administration's popularity among traditional Democratic voter groups, especially blue-collar families, indicated change was possible. Spiro Agnew's celebrated attacks in 1969 against the national news media had heartened conservatives. In the spring of 1970, the placation of Americans' uneasiness over the Vietnam War and the sudden popularity of the vice president intoxicated White House staffers.

At the same time, there was a clear difference between the aims of the national Republican Party and those of the Nixon White House. Like all other Nixon White House initiatives, building the Republican presence on Capitol Hill was seen as only a means to promote the president. A Republican Congress would give Nixon a free hand with which to create policy—or so Nixon's people believed—and to Nixon strategists that was the point. Ties to the Republican Party after Nixon's election to office were strictly a matter of practical necessity. Nixon was not so much concerned about his party as he was his own image, present and future. To this end, as the off-year elections approached, Haldeman wanted a greater Nixon presence on popular broadcast media and did not have a detailed game plan for promoting congressional candidates. He felt Communications Director Herbert Klein had failed in getting the "Nixon message" out. The idea of a split White House communications responsibility (between Klein's and Ziegler's offices) was to allow one office to spend all its time varnishing the Nixon persona. Despite rising poll figures, Haldeman was unhappy with Klein's promotion of the "new Nixon." The theme Haldeman wanted de-emphasized the cold warrior image of the 1940s and 1950s, and emphasized Nixon's role as a moderate and statesman. He and the president wanted a stronger propaganda effort, because the tactic of bullying editors, news directors, and reporters worked for only a short time. Readers and viewers tired of the mudslinging, and news people wised up to the hardball tactics. Though Agnew was the hero of the moment, voters quickly turned to the question of how they benefited from all this antagonism. Presidential aide Alexander Butterfield sent Klein a memorandum on October 7, 1969, asking for an outline of the communications director's objectives for early 1970.[2] In his answer, Klein bragged about his abilities to control what the media reported, especially the broadcast media. "For example, we have CBS doing a network radio, as well as a TV show, on the [military] draft." He also claimed to have been successful in increasing the Nixon White House presence on television shows "ranging from MEET THE PRESS, to JOHNNY CARSON, to TODAY." Klein suggested more direct contact with editors and news managers outside Washington with special emphasis on pressuring network executives.[3] This probably was not what Haldeman and Nixon wanted to hear, but it apparently satisfied them for the moment. Klein remained in his post for three more years.

Meanwhile, Nixon used his office to swing the public to his side. On January 26, 1970, he vetoed a Democratic-sponsored bill that would have provided aid to college students and to public health services through the U.S. Department of Health, Education, and Welfare. Nixon spent ten minutes on network television explaining the inflationary aspects of the $19.7 million bill before vetoing it. Mail on Capitol Hill had been ten to one in favor of the bill. After the television appearance, fifty-five thousand telegrams poured into congressional offices opposing the measure.[4] Although Nixon's people most likely helped generate part of the mail, the apparent success of the speech indicated that Nixon knew what he was doing. He had seen television's influence on viewers for more than seventeen years as vice president, private citizen, and president. Part of the discontent with Klein was that Nixon basically felt that he knew much more about media manipulation than any of his aides and it galled him that he constantly had to wait for them to come up to speed. The Klein memo pointed to Nixon's and Haldeman's heightened expectations, and the January 26 speech underscored Nixon's willingness to use network airtime to help his cause. It was impossible to control all the media in the country to make certain that Americans saw the president in only positive terms, but it was clear at the beginning of 1970 that Nixon and his two chief aides, Haldeman and John Ehrlichman, intended to control as much as possible. They would use television when they could and would try to control what reporters learned from inside the White House.

Consequently, the flow of information to reporters was controlled more intensely. Nixon wanted to shut off all communication from White House staffers to journalists. Haldeman sent a memo to Ziegler and Klein on March 9, 1970:

The president has made the decision that, as a matter of basic policy, White House staff members will not conduct briefings or make public press appearances or hold private backgrounders or appear at breakfasts and other sessions such as the Sperling Group. Obviously, there will have to be some exceptions to this rule; but this is the basic policy, and any exceptions should be approved prior to being committed. ... This policy applies to all White House members and to all press briefings. It is imperative, therefore, that both of you make sure that no such activities are scheduled and that you have the means of communication with the various White House staff offices so as to avoid any appearances or commitments of this kind in violation of the policy. This is going to take some fancy footwork on your parts, which should be implemented immediately.[5]

Leaks from White House staffers had aggravated presidents for decades, but no previous president had reasonably expected to win such a battle. Apparently Nixon did, although it was folly to expect that such an order would be followed. This paranoia over who was speaking to whom was a prelude to Watergate, because when the leaks still could not be prevented a year later, Ehrlichman aide Egil Krough called in "plumbers" who wantonly invaded homes and offices.

The Nixon-Haldeman strategy was to first outlaw leaks, then to ferret out and punish the leakers. Though wiretapping and spying had begun only a few months into the Nixon administration, instituting the prohibition on staff conversations with reporters, took the war against the press a step further and set in motion a series of decisions that would destroy the Nixon presidency. In March, many reporters moved into their new quarters in the basement of the White House in more spacious quarters but far away from the hub of presidential activity.

Nixon usually started his day by reading a lengthy news briefing prepared by speechwriter Patrick Buchanan. This summary of recent news contained commentary on who appeared to write or broadcast favorably about the president and who seemed to tilt away from the White House. Then Nixon and Haldeman—and sometimes Ehrlichman—would discuss how they wanted to control the news that day. Memos would fly and a formula for the Nixon image would emerge. So powerful were Ehrlichman and Haldeman, particularly Haldeman, that by the fall of 1971 even Nixon's longtime, faithful personal secretary Rosemary Woods had been demoted, at Haldeman's urging, to making promotional phone calls on behalf of the White House.[6]

A second part of the Nixon scheme in 1970 was to increase public opinion pressure on the national media. In response to repeated criticism from conservatives and the Nixon White House, the American Society of Newspaper Editors in December 1970 created a National Press Council to review reporting. It was a self-conscious effort by the press to police itself, but it had only partial support and no clout. The council drew the support of CBS news; CBS executive Richard Salant had been a member of the task force that recommended its establishment. A. M. Rosenthal, *New York Times* managing editor, said, "I feel very strongly that press councils are a very bad idea. ... I see no reason to cooperate with an organization whose basis we question."[7] The creation of the council suggested that Nixon and Agnew were getting to the communications moguls.

KENT STATE

History overtook Nixon in April 1970, ending the rising euphoria in the White House. On March 18, 1969, the United States conducted a bombing raid in Cambodia against North Vietnamese troops who were using Cambodia as a refuge. This covert operation had expanded the war beyond Vietnam's borders, and, though nearly four thousand similar raids were conducted over the next thirteen months, the U.S. public was kept largely uninformed about the expansion of the war. William Beecher, a reporter with the *New York Times*, revealed the secret bombing in an article that appeared in May 1969. This led to a series of wiretaps in the homes of reporters, including Beecher, to find out where the leak existed, but the nation's media did not generally follow the Beecher story, and the bombing in Cambodia remained relatively unknown outside Washington.[8] Nixon revealed officially on April 30, 1970, that the United States had been conducting raids into Cambodia. He added that the war would be expanded with the commitment of ground troops there for a short time. Protests erupted. Campuses exploded in protest, sometimes accompanied by violence or vandalism. A few days earlier NBC had picked up a chance remark Nixon had made to government employees in which he referred to violent protesters as "bums blowing up campuses." The comments were repeated in news stories after the Cambodia speech, fanning the anger. Around the country, university students stopped attending classes and instead gathered outside campus buildings, marching in unorganized throngs, and chanting slogans at the offices of bewildered administrators. Occasionally, they damaged vehicles and buildings. Throughout the country National Guardsmen and state troopers were dispersed to campuses, ostensibly to protect lives and property but usually to quell the uneasiness of townspeople and university administrators. On May 4, edgy National Guard troopers fired on a crowd of protesters at Kent State University in rural Ohio, killing four persons and injuring fifteen. Pictures of a fifteen-year-old girl, arms outstretched and sobbing over a dead body, appeared on front pages all over the country. Nixon's Vietnam policy decisions, a tragic confrontation in Ohio, and the force of seven years of pent-up public frustration unraveled the carefully cultivated Nixon image.

In the days after Kent State, it became clear that manipulation of images and press strategy would carry a presidency just so far. Nothing could erase the imprint of the pictures of the dead students. Protests met with much more sympathy from the public. More than a quarter of a million people traveled to Washington five days after the shootings to demonstrate. In the middle of the night, Nixon spontaneously wandered out to the Lincoln Memorial, where he found some protesters huddled on the steps of the monument. He explained some of his thoughts to them, but reaction to the meeting was mixed because no reporters were present and versions of the meeting's success varied according to the source. If the failed Tet offensive had been a turning point in Johnson's presidency, so was Kent State a pivotal event in Nixon's first term and the prosecution of the war. Vietnam became Nixon's war after Kent State. Nixon wrote eight years later: "Those few days after Kent State were among the darkest of my presidency. I felt utterly dejected when I read that the father of one of the dead girls had told a reporter, 'My child was not a bum.'"[9] Two students were shot at Jackson State College in Mississippi two weeks later. In June, Congress repealed the Gulf of Tonkin Resolution, passed in 1964 to give Johnson carte blanche authority to escalate the war. The symbolic gesture indicated that Congress had had enough. In August, a protester bombed a research building on the campus of the University of Wisconsin-Madison, killing a graduate student doing late-night research.

Why had Kent State so touched Americans? Thousands were dying in Vietnam, after all, and most Americans were unsympathetic to campus protesters. Timing and imagery are probably the answers. The incursion into Cambodia reminded Americans that the war still had no end in sight and that Nixon, like Johnson, had not honestly explained his military and policy decisions. Nixon had inherited a suspicious public, and the secret bombing of Cambodia now confirmed its distrust. Also, the young people killed could have been Middle Americans' brothers, sisters, children, nieces, nephews, grandchildren, or friends. There may have been differences of opinions between old and young, but the youthful infatuation with ending the war was seen by the World War II generation, in the final analysis, as a temporary aberration in the lives of ideal-istic know-nothings. No one wanted to see pictures of young people shot in an unnecessary confrontation. Visions of the four slain Kent State students and two Jackson State students reminded all concerned that, except for those who resorted to violence, protest had a proper place in America. The generation gap eased slightly and temporarily.

It would be unfair to say that Nixon did not experience remorse or that he was responsible for National Guardsmen firing their weapons hundreds of miles from Washington. But the "us versus them" mentality that had been cul-tivated for the fourteen months of his presidency hung over the entire affair. It was Nixon's and Haldeman's clear intentions to lump the media and antiwar protesters together as profane antagonists who opposed the will of most Amer-icans. Voters' real desires were reflected in Nixon's policies, the White House reasoned. But taken together, Nixon's divisive politics, his covert Cambodian policies, and his thoughtless remarks had contributed to the volatile atmo-sphere at Kent State and elsewhere.

The real surprise was that there were only two sets of shootings. Angry standoffs took place on campuses all over the country. Many classes were can-celed and spring terms abruptly concluded. At the University of Illinois in Urbana-Champaign, state police outfitted in riot gear and armed with trun-cheons and loaded rifles confronted thousands of students in the middle of a main street. The students had marched from the football stadium to the campus business district, chanting slogans and pleading with onlookers to join. Hun-dreds of armed officers met thousands of protesters in the business district. Each side held its ground, waiting for the other to move, until finally the protest broke up. An automobile backfire, a thrown rock, a slip of a trigger fin-ger, or any other sudden noise or action in those few minutes could easily have resulted in the deaths of dozens of students. Fortunately, the police and stu-dents only taunted each other before the protesters dispersed.

By the second half of 1970, the White House was on the defensive. Nixon knew that he must end the war. Publicly, he castigated those who advocated an immediate end to U.S. involvement in the war, but troop withdrawals speeded up after Kent State. By the fall of 1970, the anger against the war had abated and by the end of 1971, talk about Vietnam focused only on withdrawal of American troops. Vietnam was not the issue of the 1972 election, but Nixon's people believed from mid-1970 to November 1972 that they were under siege and that all tactics were acceptable in their fight to keep Nixon in office.

The shootings enhanced the White House commitment to cow the media. CBS News in the summer of 1970 began a policy of offering the Democrats time to respond to Nixon's speeches and other White House comments. In September, Nixon aide Charles Colson met with CBS President Frank Stanton and Board Chairman William Paley, NBC President Julian Goodman, and ABC President Leonard Goldenson and Vice President James Hagerty. Colson wrote a memo to Haldeman asserting that he had gotten the networks to back down, particularly with regard to the CBS policy of allowing comments by the loyal opposition.[10]

In November, the Republicans lost nine House seats and gained two in the Senate. Nixon's hope of augmenting his support in Congress dissipated. A long two years stretched ahead before the campaign for reelection. As luck would have it, the election would be decided by the mistakes and fumbled opportunities of the Democrats, but in late 1970 Nixon's staff believed that they were in for a titanic struggle. By the end of the year, unemployment reached its highest level in nine years.[11]

Antagonism between press and White House cut both ways. Two weeks after the fall elections, Ted Knap, Washington correspondent for Scripps-Howard Newspapers, wrote a column critical of administration press relations. He noted that a question from James Deakin, *St. Louis Post-Dispatch* correspondent, had been met by a curt response from Press Secretary Ronald Ziegler during a press briefing. Deakin wanted to know when Nixon would hold a full press conference. He had not done so in fourteen weeks, Deakin noted. Ziegler responded: "We have no press conference date set."[12]

"Bits and pieces of hostility come to the surface almost daily," Knap wrote. He noted that reporters the day before had walked out on a press conference in the Attorney General's Office because they were told they could not attribute remarks made by Jerris Leonard, assistant attorney general for civil rights. The Freedom of Information Committee of Sigma Delta Chi, a professional journalism society, had issued a statement criticizing Nixon's lack of press conferences. Nixon had held only eleven in twenty-one months, Knap noted. Agnew's constant attacks on the press did not help, Knap added.[13] The public had now been drawn into the argument by both sides.

But Kent State had further aggravated White House paranoia, and the illegal wiretaps that had marked the first fifteen months of the Nixon presidency were greatly expanded in the summer of 1970. Haldeman developed a plan to coordinate and systematize the illegal acts. He assigned an aide, Tom Huston, to develop a new system of domestic intelligence gathering. A committee—the Intelligence Evaluation Committee, composed of the Central Intelligence Agency, FBI, National Security Agency, and White House leaders—met in the White House to develop a comprehensive approach to undercutting opposition to the war and spying on antiwar protesters. The plan included opening mail, tapping telephones without warrants, breaking into homes and offices, and spying on students.[14]

DESEGREGATION

In the early 1970s Nixon was forced to deal with the aftermath of comprehensive legislation passed in the 1960s under Lyndon Johnson and liberal interpretations of the Constitution with regard to inclusiveness in the country. Forced busing began to infiltrate the agendas of Northern school districts as well as districts in the South. Nixon sent Ehrlichman a memorandum in January 1972 laying out his philosophy on desegregation. It said in part, "I am convinced that while legal segregation is totally wrong, forced integration of housing or education is just as wrong."[15] This seemed to capture the attitude of most Northerners. De jure segregation held the stigma of second-class citizenship, superior white attitudes, pillowcases with eyeholes and bedsheets as wearing apparel, and brutality. Somehow, ghettos in the inner cities separated from white neighborhoods and suburbs seemed to make perfect sense. When court-ordered integration of schools through busing came to Northern urban centers, the public looked to the White House for loopholes. Desegregation continued under Nixon's watch, but the White House pursued a fairly low-key support of busing and most of the confrontations took place later in the decade under Gerald Ford's and Jimmy Carter's administrations.

Nixon tried unsuccessfully to win legislative support in 1970 and 1971 for welfare reform and public housing initiatives. Conservatives within his own party opposed many White House proposals, and the Nixon coterie found it difficult to deal with congressional Democrats, who were suspicious and uncooperative with the "imperial White House." Democrats held majorities in both houses throughout Nixon's tenure.

The Middle East continued to be a world scourge in the early 1970s. France had sold fighter jets to Libya in 1970, and Nixon was pressured to keep a balance in the region. The Soviet Union was still a world force, and Nixon had to take into account the U.S. need for oil, the strategic value of the Suez Canal, Israeli and American Jewish interests, Arab nationalism, the increasingly violent but popular (among Arabs) Palestine Liberation Organization (PLO), and the Cold War world strategy of opposing Soviet intervention in regional strife. Nixon relied on Kissinger to negotiate an uncertain calm in the region, but eventually the competing interests brought the region to its fourth and final conflict of the twentieth century in October 1973.

Inflation and unemployment increased in 1971, and Nixon later tried wage and price controls briefly as a method of regulating the economy. As always, artificial constraints failed and the economy stagnated. Strategic Arms Limitation Talks (SALT) resulted in an agreement with the Soviet Union to reduce nuclear arms stockpiles, though only slightly. Tensions between Indians and Pakistanis deteriorated into war in late 1971, with the Indians eventually routing Pakistani forces.

While Nixon continued to pursue moderate domestic and international policies, the determining question of the success or failure of his first term seemed to be how he approached the war in Southeast Asia. The Kent State shootings and the revelations of U.S. incursions in Cambodia seemed to cast a shadow over the White House, but Nixon's advisors were not politically astute enough to recognize that public indignation has a short shelf life. What the public generally wanted was an end to the conflict, and as troop removals accelerated in 1971 and 1972, the voting public forgot about Cambodia. Nevertheless, the White House psyche had been damaged and the plotting within the Oval Office and West Wing would undermine the public successes of 1969, 1970, and 1971. The issues of the day around the globe and in the country demanded Nixon's full attention and energy. Yet, time after time he wasted his talents brooding over press reports, his place in history, and his opponents. Polls in mid-1971 showed that he was trailing both Senators Edward Kennedy and Edmund Muskie among likely voters. In the spring of 1971 a confrontation over a CBS news program signaled a new level of White House paranoia and anger with the world of journalism.

NOTES

1. Theodore White, *The Making of the President 1972* (New York: Atheneum, 1973), 59.

2. Alexander P. Butterfield, memorandum to Herbert Klein, October 7, 1969, Klein Papers, Box 2, Memos to the President folder.

3. Klein to Nixon, memorandum, October 9, 1969, 1–3, Klein Papers, Box 2.

4. Joseph C. Spear, *Presidents and the Press: The Nixon Legacy* (Cambridge, Mass.: MIT Press, 1984), 88.

5. Haldeman to Klein and Ziegler, memo, March 9, 1970, Klein Papers, Box 2, Staff Memos folder.

6. Stanley I. Kutler, *The Wars of Watergate: The Last Crisis of Richard Nixon* (New York: Knopf, 1990), 84–85.

7. Associated Press wire copy in Ziegler files, Box 7, miscellaneous.

8. Michael A. Genovese, *The Nixon Presidency: Power and Politics in Turbulent Times* (New York: Greenwood, 1990), 124–25.

9. Richard Nixon, *The Memoirs of Richard Nixon* (New York: Grosset & Dunlop, 1978), 457.

10. Spear, *Presidents and the Press*, 142–43.

11. Nixon, *The Memoirs of Richard Nixon*, 497.

12. Ted Knapp, "Press sore at President," *Washington Daily News*, November 18, 1970.

13. Ibid.

14. Genovese, *The Nixon White House*, 126–27; for Nixon's version of the Huston plan, see Nixon, *The Memoirs of Richard Nixon*, 474–75.

15. Nixon, *The Memoirs of Richard Nixon*, 443.

Chapter 3

The Break-In

Despite the loss of seats for the GOP in the 1970 congressional elections and the aftermath of the Kent State shootings, the White House viewed President Nixon's second two years in office as an opportunity for progress in world and domestic issues and for headway in its quest to silence media criticism. In January 1971 in an evening telecast from the White House library, Nixon answered questions from four of the most powerful broadcasters on national television: Eric Severeid of the Columbia Broadcasting System (CBS), John Chancellor of the National Broadcasting Company (NBC), Howard K. Smith of the American Broadcasting Company (ABC), and Nancy Dickerson of the Public Broadcasting System (PBS). The interview went well for Nixon. The questions were not terribly probing, and the exchange was polite with Nixon looking well versed and in control, leading Americans to think the president's relationship with the press in general was a good one and leaving the White House inner circle with the feeling that criticism had been adequately contained.

But just a month later, a very different kind of telecast, "The Selling of the Pentagon," appeared on the screen. On February 23, 1971, CBS aired the documentary, which detailed how taxpayer dollars were being spent to promote the public image of the military. It illustrated how money was spent for air shows, public military maneuvers, and junkets for congressmen. The program was rebroadcast on March 23. At the end of the rebroadcast, Secretary of Defense Melvin Laird and Vice President Spiro Agnew were given time to present opposing views. CBS News President Richard S. Salant then responded to their criticism. The White House did not dominate the telecast or the rebroadcast, as had been the case with the January interview. To the contrary, the administration was portrayed as a shill for the military, and suddenly the Nixon image makers were in a panic. "The Selling of the Pentagon" was controversial because it suggested that the military was propagandizing the public at taxpayer expense, a message that had long been argued by opponents of the war in Vietnam. It also seemed to aggravate the divisions between the World War II and baby-boom generations. But in the White House, the president's inner circle also saw the documentary as another example of the liberal media's intentional distortion of the news and one more attack on Nixon. This time, the White House counterattacks against CBS had plenty of support from Congress on both sides of the aisle, because many influential congressmen, including the chair of the Armed Services Committee, were depicted as toadies for the military and the defense industry.

In a speech in Boston on March 18, Agnew assailed the program and linked it with two earlier CBS documentaries on the invasion of Haiti in 1966 and on "Hunger in America" (1968). The Haiti documentary was never aired, but Agnew lumped the three news specials together anyway, alleging that they showed a pattern of biased reporting. "Considering the serious charges leveled recently by the CBS television news organization against the public affairs activities of the Department of Defense, the matter of the network's own record in the field of documentary-making can no longer be brushed under the rug of national media indifference," the vice president told his audience at Boston's Middlesex Club, a bastion of sympathetic Republicans. Agnew said that the same unidentified producer was involved in the filming of all three documentaries and that, in many cases, interviews were staged or CBS cooperated with persons who were breaking the law. Agnew expanded his invective to include all national media, which he claimed "cloak themselves in a special immunity to criticism."[1] Agnew closed by saying that he was not trying to "intimidate a network or any segment of the national news media in its effort to enhance the people's right to know." However, the right to know belongs to the people, Agnew added, and "they are entitled to a fair and full accounting of the truth, and nothing but the truth, by those who exercise great influence with their consent."[2]

The Special Subcommittee on Investigations of the House Interstate and Foreign Commerce Committee launched an inquiry into "The Selling of the Pentagon." The subcommittee subpoenaed CBS President Frank Stanton on April 7 and then, after objections from CBS lawyers, narrowed the scope of the subpoena request and reissued it on May 26. The subpoena demanded that Stanton turn over "film, work prints, outtakes, sound-tape recordings, written scripts, and/or transcripts utilized in connection with 'The Selling of the Pentagon.'"[3] CBS's lawyers, Wilmer, Cutler, and Pickering of Washington, D.C., sent a confidential memo to Stanton citing several legal cases establishing that broadcast media were just as clearly covered by the First Amendment as print media, adding that each subpoena "has an unconstitutional chilling effect upon the exercise of First Amendment rights."[4]

CBS's lawyers also wrote:

Whether or not the Subcommittee can devise constitutional legislation regulating the manner in which broadcasters must edit the news, the Subcommittee cannot, in our opinion, enforce the present subpoena in aid of that objective. ... To demand that CBS supply unedited material so that the government can review its editing judgments would have an unconstitutionally chilling effect upon the First Amendment Rights of CBS and all other broadcast journalists, and ultimately the public's right to see and hear vigorous and critical comment on public affairs.[5]

In a continuing effort to stem White House and congressional criticism, CBS carried a special report, "Perspective: The Selling of the Pentagon" on April 18, during which persons representing all sides of the issue discussed their support for or concerns with the documentary. Appearing on the show to contradict the documentary's findings were Arthur Sylvester, former assistant secretary of defense for public affairs, and General S. L. A. Marshall, a military commentator and historian. Senator William Fulbright, D-Arkansas, and Adam Yarmolinsky, special assistant to Lyndon Johnson's secretary of defense, Robert McNamara, supported the documentary's message.

CBS refused to provide the subcommittee with most of the materials, but on April 30 it turned over "some general information about the program."[6] Stanton appeared before the subcommittee on June 24. He told the members:

The chilling effect of both the subpoena and the inquiry itself is plain beyond all question. If newsmen are told that their notes, films and tapes will be subject to compulsory process so that the government can determine whether the news has been satisfactorily edited, the scope, nature and vigor of their news gathering and reporting activities will inevitably be curtailed.[7]

Stanton said that he was not necessarily objecting to the government's right to subpoena a journalist and unpublished notes, but that, on advice of counsel, and based upon the conviction that "a fundamental principle of a free society is at stake," he could not turn over any specific materials in this particular case. He also told the subcommittee that he would not answer any questions relating to the preparation of "The Selling of the Pentagon" or any other news or documentary program and that news organizations, educational groups, and civic and religious groups from all over the country supported CBS.[8]

The controversial documentary had once again focused the public's attention on how national media covered government. The effect of "The Selling of the Pentagon" controversy was twofold. First, it aroused the networks once again to battle the administration. After Agnew's attacks in 1969, ABC, CBS, and NBC had pulled back precipitously in their criticism of Nixon and his administration, as was evidenced by the January joint interview in the White House and by the support from CBS for the National News Council.

However, Agnew's comments and the subcommittee's investigation convinced the networks, particularly CBS, that cooperation and conciliation were the wrong paths. It was one thing to criticize and insult, but quite another to require media to allow government officials to review the editing and creative process associated with a filmed documentary. CBS clearly had had enough. Its actions after March 1971 indicated that it was through trying to compromise with the Nixon White House.

Second, the Democrat-led congressional subcommittee's actions signaled some sympathy from across the aisle for the White House's attacks on the media. Democrats controlled all committees and subcommittees; yet, here was a subcommittee essentially in league with Nixon and Agnew to cow a national network. After early 1971 and until the details of Watergate became known in 1973, official Washington, including the Democrats, were increasingly reluctant to stand beside the media when the White House lashed out. None of the spying, eavesdropping, and dirty tricks had come to light by June 1971, so the public also sided with the White House, particularly those segments of the public unhappy with television's depiction of the war. Nixon's battle with the press escalated until the summer of 1971, with the public leaning toward the anti-media camp.

In April 1971 Ehrlichman told Salant that CBS White House correspondent Dan Rather was lazy, a remark that many journalists interpreted as an attempt to get Rather fired, which Ehrlichman denied. The remark had been made when Ehrlichman traveled to New York to conduct an interview at the CBS studios. He met Salant at a nearby restaurant while having breakfast with his interviewer, John Hart. Ehrlichman told Salant that he rarely heard from any of CBS's reporters, but that they were consistently critical of Nixon's domestic policies. According to Ehrlichman's own account of the conversation, he described Rather as "lazy." Salant told Haldeman that Rather was a good reporter. Two months later, newspapers began reporting that Ehrlichman tried to get Rather fired. Ehrlichman claimed that was not his intention at all, but that he was only responding to a question from Salant. Years later, Erlichman wrote that in 1978 Rather intervened to create trouble for him with his parole officer and another CBS reporter told him then that he, too, felt that Rather was lazy.[9]

About the time the CBS documentary aired, Nixon and Chief of Staff H.R. Haldeman made a fateful decision. A taping system was turned on in the Oval Office. It was voice-activated, meaning that when anyone in the room spoke, the system began recording. Later, taping devices were installed in a Nixon office in the Executive Office Building, at Camp David, in the Cabinet Room, and inside various telephones in the White House and Camp David. Only Nixon, Haldeman, Haldeman aide Alexander Butterfield, and four Secret Service agents knew about the system. It was a renovated version of what Lyndon Johnson had installed in the Oval Office seven years earlier. John F. Kennedy and Franklin D. Roosevelt had also secretly taped a few conversations in the Oval Office through hidden tape recorders, but Nixon's system was far more pervasive than any before it. In all, between February 1971 and July 1973, more than 3,700 hours of conversations were recorded on 950 tapes. After Nixon's resignation, the tapes were stored at the National Archives II in Arlington, Virginia, and then in College Park, Maryland. By 1991, only the 12½ hours of tapes offered in the Watergate trials had been made available to the public and, by 1999, only 418 hours. Following an $18 million settlement between the government and the Nixon family in 2000, it was expected that by 2003 nearly all of the 3,500 hours would be available. About 200 hours of the tapes were blank. It would be a long time before the full truth about the Nixon White House was known, but the tapes made certain that it would eventually all come out.[10]

Why did Nixon begin taping? He wrote later that he wanted an accurate historical record of his administration and that having someone in a room transcribing conversations inhibited free discussion. The decision to reinstall the Johnson system in February 1971 resulted from criticism of the U.S. incursion into Laos, Nixon wrote. "Such an objective record might also be useful to the extent that any President feels vulnerable to revisionist histories."[11] In truth, the installation of the taping system is one more example of the paranoia that increasingly dominated the mindset in the White House. That the installation of the taping system was nearly concurrent with the airing of "The Selling of the Pentagon" seems not coincidental, but the simultaneous events provide two examples of the White House orientation. Nixon trusted no one in or out of the White House by the spring of 1971. The taping was a symptom of an increasingly troubled atmosphere. In fact, by the fall of 1971, Haldeman, Ehrlichman, Colson, and Larry Higby, a Haldeman aide, were all secretly taping all their phone conversations.[12]

The paranoia soon manifested itself again in another showdown. Just before Stanton appeared before the congressional subcommittee, another historical confrontation would have even more serious implications.

PENTAGON PAPERS

On June 12, 1971, in a grand Rose Garden ceremony, Nixon hosted the wedding of his daughter Tricia to her high school sweetheart, Edward Cox. Obviously, the marriage of the eldest daughter was one of the highlights of the Nixon experience in the White House. The family enjoyed the day thoroughly, probably one of the few days of Nixon's last three years in office that the Nixons in later years remembered fondly.

The next morning, however, the mood changed. Accompanying a picture and account of the wedding on the front page of the *New York Times* was another story under the headline, "Vietnam Archive: Pentagon Study Traces 3 Decades of Growing U.S. Involvement." The newspaper had broken the story of inner governmental maneuvering during the conflict. The story was based upon a report begun by Johnson's defense secretary, Robert McNamara, in 1967. Using material from the top secret report, the article explained how Johnson had misled Congress and the public about casualty figures, government strategy, and U.S. troop involvement in Vietnam. A disgruntled former McNamara aide, Daniel Ellsberg, had leaked the information. Government lawyers sought an injunction in New York federal District Court to stop further installments of the series in the *Times*. The *Washington Post* and other newspapers then received copies of the Pentagon Papers and began publishing articles. They, too, were served with injunctions. On June 30, 1971, seventeen days after the first installment appeared, the U.S. Supreme Court ruled against the government, six to three, and the publication of the articles resumed. Nixon's secretary of defense, Melvin Laird, told Nixon that 95 percent of the Pentagon Papers could have been declassified. According to Nixon's memoirs, the president insisted that the principle of government secrecy, especially during war, was involved and that he was obligated to challenge the release of the Pentagon Papers by any news organization, though none of the information dealt with policy decisions made during his time in office.[13]

However, the Oval Office tape recordings, released in 1996, indicate a different Nixon reaction. In the weeks immediately after the articles appeared, Nixon met on several occasions and plotted with White House advisors to undertake a number of possible countermeasures to the revelations. They included: (1) use of information from the papers to "blackmail" Johnson (a suggestion from Haldeman); (2) at Haldeman's suggestion again, infiltration of peace groups to show that antiwar activists continually stole top secret documents; (3) a campaign against Ellsberg to tie him publicly to a communist group; (4) trying Ellsberg in the press. "Everything that there is on the investigation get it out. Leak it out. We want to destroy him in the press. Press. Is that clear?" Nixon demanded of Attorney General John Mitchell and Henry Kissinger, assistant to the president for national security affairs, in the Oval Office; (5) Plotting a possible break-in at the Brookings Institute, a Washington liberal think tank, where Nixon's people suspected that more details from the Pentagon Papers were being kept; (6) Creation of a "plumber's unit" to fix information leaks from the White House.

Egil Krogh, an aide to John Ehrlichman, counsel to the president for domestic affairs, headed the plumbers. Krogh recruited Kissinger aide David Young, former CIA agent E. Howard Hunt, and former FBI agent G. Gordon Liddy. They occupied an office in the basement of the White House and in September traveled to Los Angeles to break into the office of Ellsberg's Beverly Hills psychiatrist, Lewis Fielding, to gain personal information about Ellsberg.[14] Haldeman's notes, published in book form by his wife after Haldeman's death, make no mention of the illegal acts that Nixon or Haldeman proposed at these meetings. There are references to the Pentagon Papers, but no suggestion of underhanded retaliations.[15]

Presidential aide Charles Colson spent only four pages of his memoirs on the Pentagon Papers and mentioned in passing that Nixon ordered that anything necessary must be done to stop the leaks, but offered no particulars.[16] Ehrlichman's memoirs devoted only two pages to the Pentagon Papers and Haldeman's six. They both claimed that Kissinger was the person who really wanted to act aggressively toward release of the papers, because Kissinger had helped formulate policy for McNamara and was mentioned prominently in the papers. Neither Colson nor Ehrlichman mentioned any illegal acts.[17] But the tapes indicate that Ehrlichman directed the break-in and reported it to Nixon with some relish. "We had one little operation. It's been aborted out in Los Angeles, which, I think, is better that you don't know about. But we've got some dirty tricks underway. It may pay off. We've planted a bunch of stuff with columnists [about Ellsberg and his lawyer]," Ehrlichman told Nixon. Ehrlichman also said that one of the columnists was Jerald terHorst, President Gerald Ford's press secretary in 1974.[18] Two days later Ehrlichman proposed that White House operatives break in to the National Archives to get more papers.[19]

Though the burglary at Fielding's office and the Plumbers Unit became public knowledge during the 1973 Senate Watergate Committee hearings, until 1996 we essentially had only the White House's version of what occurred during the aftermath of the publication of the Pentagon Papers. This particular series of incidents is a case study of how Watergate-era events have been seen in a different light since the 1996 release of the 201 hours of so-called Abuse of Government Power tapes. We now have a different feel of what was happening in the Nixon inner circles. It is not so much that the information is all that different, but the attitudes and the covert activities are seen for what they are—extensions of White House overheated anxieties, while the conversations underline the rampant vindictiveness. "We have got to go after everyone who is a member of this conspiracy," Nixon told Ehrlichman and Haldeman two days after the Supreme Court ruling, according to a tape released in 1999.[20]

There is more to be learned from a reexamination of the Pentagon Papers case. Pieces of a complex puzzle fit more evenly after the post-1996 examination. The suppression of the papers, even for a few weeks, was a monumental event in media history. It was the first time in nearly two hundred years that newspaper stories were withheld through prior restraint. Always in the past, courts and disgruntled parties had acted after the fact, suing the publication once the information was published. Though the Pentagon Papers court case did not seem to have set an unhealthy precedent for the remainder of the twentieth century, judging from the lack of prior restraint exercised in ensuing years, it did establish a legal precedent for events that could follow in the twenty-first century and beyond.

Aside from that, it stirred the White House to a third level of antipress feeling. Agnew's verbal attacks in late 1969, the Kent State shootings in May 1970, and finally the release of the Pentagon Papers (soon after "The Selling of the Pentagon" aired) had each, in its own way, driven the White House to increasing depths of suspicion and paranoia. Something seemed to come loose after the Pentagon Papers episode. The White House cast aside restraints on underhanded activities and began a systematic effort to undercut "enemies." The plumbers and their break-in at Fielding's office were clear examples of that. Nixon claimed later that the plumbers were disbanded after their burglary, but the concept remained. "You're going to be my Lord High Executioner from now on," Nixon told Haldeman days after the first article was published.[21]

The Pentagon Papers case injected into the White House two problematic characters: Hunt and Liddy. Both were egocentric, unpredictable operatives whose involvement in White House internal dirty tricks brought unpredictability to the already misguided covert operations. Every person who came into contact with those two at the White House would regret it.

Thus, the Pentagon Papers not only brought the press and the president to a flash point again, but also created a constitutional clash between government and media unnecessarily and triggered a final mindset that led to a march toward the Watergate break-in.

Nixon became even more uncommunicative with reporters. He held seventeen press conferences in the twenty-seven months before the Pentagon Papers case broke, but in the next twelve months he held only six. After the Watergate investigation began to tighten the noose, Nixon used press conferences on national television to make a case for himself, so the rate increased as Nixon's troubles escalated. But the time period when Nixon went silent was the twelve months between the Pentagon Papers case and the Watergate burglary.

Behind the scenes in the summer of 1971, the Nixon people immediately enmeshed themselves in increasingly reckless acts. For several months, operatives under Haldeman's direction had been trying to find out who was leaking information to columnist Jack Anderson. In July 1971, just days after the adverse Supreme Court ruling in the Pentagon Papers case, FBI and Defense Department officials seized Anderson's telephone records, according to journalist Joseph Spear. At the same time, the plumbers investigated, wiretapped, and followed Anderson and his associates. In January 1972, the CIA also began following Anderson and his staff around because Anderson had reported that Dita Beard, a lobbyist for International Telephone and Telegraph, had suggested in a 1971 memo that ITT underwrite $400,000 of the cost of the 1972 Republican National Convention in exchange for the settlement of several antitrust suits. The Justice Department had agreed to the settlements in July 1971. Twenty CIA agents as well as the White House plumbers followed Anderson's staff and sources, while the FBI tapped their phones. Spear, who obtained the CIA files through a Freedom of Information request, was one of the persons followed by the CIA.[22]

On July 6, Nixon also ordered surveillance on Massachusetts Senator Edward Kennedy, presumably in anticipation of Kennedy's running against Nixon the next year. "Do you have Kennedy—find the man, you have Kennedy?" Nixon asked Haldeman during an Oval Office conversation that day. Haldeman replied, "Yeah. This morning, we made a decision to get a guy going." Nixon responded, "Certainly. Just one? He'll be on it full time?"[23]

Another journalist who was pursued by the FBI at the behest of the White House during the summer of 1971 was CBS correspondent Daniel Schorr, one of the journalists whom the White House had targeted as an "enemy" before Nixon even took office. On August 20, an FBI agent met Schorr at his CBS office. The agent told Schorr told that he had been assigned to do a background interview with Schorr in anticipation of Schorr's being offered an appointment with the government. Schorr did not wish to work for the Nixon Administration and found it incredible that anyone in the White House would be interested in hiring him. The head of the New York FBI office had called CBS president Salant earlier that morning to tell him that Schorr needed to be cleared in three days for a possible appointment. CBS decided not to pursue a story about the FBI background checks on Schorr, but kept the discussion in-house. When the *Washington Post* in November 1971 broke a story about the phony job and FBI background check of Schorr, a Senate Committee investigation resulted.

The parties involved in sending the FBI to Schorr's office were recorded later bragging that the pretext of wanting to hire Schorr was a sham. Eighteen months later, Nixon told Haldeman and secretary Rose Mary Woods, "As a matter of fact, you're quite aware of the fact that when we were looking into him [Schorr]—and we were looking into him—it was not for a job." "That's right," Haldeman responded. Then Nixon continued, "Actually, we were looking into him, Rose, because of national security."[24]

The dispute between the press and Nixon became ever more public as the months went by. In December 1971 editors at both the *Washington Post* and the *New York Times* called for an end to honoring administration requests to talk to reporters on background. "Background" means that the speaker has an agreement to provide information to reporters that will help them to understand better the issues or events occurring, but the reporters are not allowed to quote the source or use any specific information for a story. Both newspapers claimed that the Nixon administration was abusing the use of background sourcing and their reporters were no longer to honor such requests. The White House Correspondents Association issued a statement in opposition to the *Post*'s and the *Times*'s positions. The association statement said that background sourcing should be avoided, but reporters must abide by the rules when background discussions are initiated.[25] The dispute soon died, but it is indicative of the mistrust that had developed by the end of 1971.

CHINA TRIP

As Nixon licked his wounds over the Pentagon Papers, Kissinger traveled to Asia on July 11 to plan one of the most momentous events of the first term. On July 15, Nixon told the nation in a televised address that Kissinger had arranged for a presidential visit to China sometime before May 1972 (it turned out to be in February). The United States had had almost no public dealings with the People's Republic of China since communist forces led by Mao Zedong had won the Chinese civil war in 1949 and driven the Chiang Kai-shek Nationalists to the island of Formosa (later named Taiwan). The United States had seen to it that the Nationalists were still the China representatives on the United Nations

Security Council. Because they were bitter enemies, Mao's and Chiang's continuing roles as leaders of the two nations had been a major impediment to normal Chinese-U.S. relations. The impact of the Nixon announcement was almost incalculable. Reporters and the public alike had expected some routine report on Vietnam. No one was prepared for Nixon's bombshell that night.

The virulent brand of Marxism in mainland China during the twenty-two years of Mao's rule had isolated the Chinese from the Western world, particularly the United States. Diplomatic contacts and overtures to China through third-party countries had been secretly underway for over two years. Three months earlier, a U.S. table tennis team had visited the People's Republic of China in a symbolic gesture of potential closer relations. Trade controls with China and travel restrictions had been eased in 1970. Many observers sensed a thawing of relations, but a visit by the president in a few short months to a country that had had almost no U.S. visitors for two decades? It was unimaginable. And yet it was brilliant. It was exactly what Nixon needed to draw attention away from the bitter struggles in Washington and the combat in Vietnam.

Nixon would fly to China, looking as presidential as he ever had, while voters prepared to go to the polls to vote in the presidential primaries. An avowed anticommunist who had built a career by hounding Alger Hiss to prison and by jawing with Soviet Premier Nikita Khrushchev inside a kitchen exhibit in 1959, Nixon had clearly demonstrated his Cold War credentials. He could open the door to China without hearing a chorus of recriminations about his being soft on communism, while Johnson or Kennedy, for instance, did not have that luxury. Little was known in the United States about China in 1971, and Americans were curious about the country, which had been largely ignored for nearly a quarter of a century. It was clear that this would be a momentous step. The nation with the world's largest population would be resuming some normal diplomatic relations with the richest nation in the world.

The visit to China signaled that the Chinese were convinced that the U.S. role in Vietnam was coming to an end (there would be less than 70,000 U.S. troops in Vietnam by May 1972, compared with 500,000 three years earlier). It indicated that the communists were realistic enough to understand that they could not progress culturally and economically without normal relations with the United States. It showed that the United States recognized that China would someday be a powerful economic and political force in the world. Not to mention that there were over a billion people in China who had never used American laundry detergents, drunk American soft drinks, watched American-made televisions, or worn American-made sweatshirts and who might soon be introduced to these wonders.

Not all peoples were pleased with the announcement, of course. The Taiwan government accurately gauged that its days as an influence in world affairs were numbered and that the United States was finally giving up on its old ally, Chiang Kai-shek. It worried further that an invasion from the mainland might soon result (an eventuality that still had not occurred thirty years later but one that still worried Taiwan). The always suspicious Soviets viewed this thaw in relations as an ominous portent for the future of Soviet-style communism, a correct fear as history has shown, and the South Vietnamese government had to wonder just where it stood in its battle against communism.

On February 17, 1972, Nixon flew in Air Force One to Peking (later known as Beijing). While the other presidential candidates slogged through snowdrifts in freezing New Hampshire ringing doorbells, Nixon visited the Great Wall of China, while the miracle of satellite-aided international television flashed pictures on small screens to two hundred million Americans back home. Americans saw scenes from across China depicting a happy people content with their roles as proletarians struggling against the vast capitalistic conspiracy in the West. Nixon sat at grand banquets with the leaders of China and talked world peace.

With the winding down of the Vietnam War and a more peaceful relationship in China, Americans saw clearly for the first time the possibility of a conclusion to the great international controversies of the second half of the twentieth century. The Chinese could hope for a more stable Asia, where turmoil had existed for all of the twentieth century and most of the nineteenth. Nixon's visit promised a better world for future generations and a new world order for the twenty-first century. Indeed, that potential was soon partially fulfilled. The Chinese excursion also portrayed the Nixon that could have been, had he only spent more time employing his natural diplomatic skills instead of darkly plotting against his critics.

The visit to China was certainly the pinnacle of the Nixon years. All the Nixon people emphasized China in their written recollections. The president spent fifty pages of his memoirs recounting the trip. The sojourn and the nearly concurrent U.S. disengagement from Vietnam convinced many Americans that they had misjudged Nixon and that the press was a monolithic, liberal institution that had mistreated the president. The world was Nixon's in the winter of 1972 and all the negative polls turned upward, but the roller-coaster presidency would turn downward again just four months later. By mid-1973, hardly anyone talked about the trip to China anymore. The arrogant and careless White House plotters would finally stumble fatally in June 1972, and two reporters would be the cause of the fall.

On June 17, 1972, five burglars illegally entered the office area in the Watergate hotel-office-apartment complex just three blocks from the White House. Four of the men were of Cuban extraction—Bernard L. Barker, Eugenio R. Martinez, Frank Sturgis, and Virgilio R. Gonzales—and the fifth was former CIA agent James W. McCord, who was chief of security for the Committee to Re-Elect the President. The five entered through the basement and broke into the offices of the headquarters of the Democratic National Committee. They were hoping to adjust listening devices that had been installed three weeks earlier. Unknown to the public for several months, the men had been hired by the White House. Hunt and Liddy watched the operation from a hotel nearby. Tape had been placed on the latch of one of the doors that guarded the basement stairway, so that the door would remain open and the burglars could retreat through that stairway. A guard on his rounds noticed the tape and removed it. The burglars then replaced the tape, and when the security man noticed the tape again, he investigated. The White House's paranoia, arrogance, and clumsiness had finally backfired. Watergate was a "third-rate burglary," as Ziegler described it the following week, but it was also the out-cropping of a stupid and inept approach to national politics and an election that had already, more or less, been decided. The episode had all the elements of the underhanded acts since Nixon had taken office with one added ingredient: someone got caught and, because of two reporters and a persistent judge, the truth would come out this time.

NOTES

1. Associated Press wire story, March 18, 1971, and "Address by the Vice President, Middlesex Club," Boston, Massachusetts, March 18, 1971, Ronald Ziegler Papers, CBS files, Box 18.

2. Statement of the Vice President, Middlesex Club, Boston, Massachusetts, March 18, 1971, 9, Ziegler Papers, CBS file, Box 18.

3. Legal advice from Wilmer, Cutler & Pickering Law Offices, Washington, D.C., to CBS, June 15, 1971, p. 1, Ziegler Papers, CBS file, Box 18.

4. Ibid.

5. Ibid., 4–5.

6. Frank Stanton, subcommittee testimony of June 24, 1971, p. 1, Ziegler Papers, CBS file, Box 18.

7. Ibid., 4.

8. Ibid., 5–7.

9. John Ehrlichman, *Witness to Power: The Nixon Years* (New York: Simon & Schuster, 1982), 277–283.

10. For a complete listing and background on the Nixon Tapes, see "Presidential Records and Historic Materials Available for Research from the Nixon Presidential Materials Staff," National Archives II guide, College Park, Md. See also Stanley I. Kutler, *Abuse of Power: The New Nixon Tapes* (New York: The Free Press, 1997), xiii–xxiii. Kutler's persistence in the court system is largely responsible for a 1996 agreement that brought about extensive release of the tapes.

11. Nixon, *The Memoirs of Richard Nixon*, 500–01.

12. Theodore White, *Breach of Faith: The Fall of Richard Nixon* (New York: Atheneum, 1975), 151.

13. Nixon, *The Memoirs of Richard Nixon*, 508–12.

14. See Nixon, Haldeman, and Ehrlichman, taped Oval Office conversation, June 17, 1971; Nixon and Haldeman, taped Oval Office conversation, June 23, 1971; Nixon and Charles Colson, conversation, White House telephone, June 29, 1971; Nixon, Mitchell,

and Kissinger, Oval Office conversation, June 30, 1971; Nixon, Haldeman, Mitchell, Kissinger, Ziegler, and Laird, Oval Office conversation, June 30, 1971; and Nixon, Haldeman, Colson, and Ehrlichman, Oval Office conversation, July 1, 1971.

15. See H.R. Haldeman, *The Haldeman Diaries* (New York: G. P. Putnam's Sons, 1994), 299–312.

16. See Charles Colson, *Born Again* (Old Tappan, N.J.: Chosen Books, 1976), 58–62.

17. Ehrlichman, *Witness to Power*, 300–02. H. R. Haldeman, *The Ends of Power* (New York Times Books, 1978), 110–15.

18. Nixon and Ehrlichman, Oval Office conversation, Nixon Tapes, September 8, 1971.

19. Ibid.

20. Nixon, Haldeman, and Ehrlichman, Oval Office taped conversation, July 2, 1971.

21. Ibid., 111.

22. Joseph C. Spear, *Presidents and the Press: The Nixon Legacy* (Cambridge, Mass.: MIT Press, 1984), 134–39.

23. Nixon and Haldeman, Oval Office conversation, Nixon Tapes, July 6, 1971.

24. Nixon, Haldeman, and Rose Mary Woods, Oval Office conversation, January 10, 1973, Nixon Tapes.

25. Statement of December 30, 1971, White House Correspondents Association, Ziegler Papers, Box 18, Backgrounders file.

Chapter 4

The 1972 Election

Candidates lined up for the 1972 primaries, but all of them developed their own problems and so, despite the deadly scandal that was simmering in the White House, the presidential election proved to be mundane and lopsided. Polls in mid-1971 indicated that Nixon was vulnerable—his approval rating had dropped below 50 percent by late spring, with Maine Senator Edmund Muskie leading by as many as eight percentage points in head-to-head polling samples. Two candidates from Nixon's own party declared early in 1972. On the left was antiwar California Congressman Paul McCloskey, and on the right was conservative Ohio Congressman John Ashbrook. Both were easily swept aside.

Nixon's decision to leave his name on the ballot in New Hampshire by the January 5 deadline was taken as a declaration of his candidacy, but he was uncertain what to do about Agnew. In September 1971, the president told his chief of staff, H. R. Haldeman, that he saw Agnew as a "liability." He needed to indicate his support for Agnew publicly to stop press speculation and blunt the "extreme right," Nixon added, but he would not decide until later whether to retain Agnew.[1] By the time the decision to keep the vice president was made at the convention in the summer of 1972, it was clear that Nixon would be an easy winner and that Agnew's presence made no difference. It would be better to keep the vice president and avoid any discord on the right, Nixon reasoned. Agnew probably did not know until much later how close he came to being dropped from the ticket. As events unfolded, he probably would have been better off leaving national politics in 1972.

The reelection organization was the Committee to Re-Elect the President or CRP, promptly renamed CREEP by the headline writers. Normally, such committees merely adopted the names of the candidates, such as the Wilson Re-Election Committee or the Eisenhower Re-Election Committee. Nixon's campaign became the Committee to Re-Elect the President because Haldeman's marketing research indicated that people reacted badly to Nixon's name, something about the "Nix." He devised a committee and a campaign that incorporated the term "president," rather than "Nixon."

Nixon's attorney general and his old law partner in New York, John Mitchell, resigned in January 1972 to head up CREEP, and Secretary of Commerce Maurice Stans became finance committee chair. Stans helped raise fifty-two million dollars for the campaign. When the Plumbers Unit was disbanded in fall of 1971, G. Gordon Liddy, was named head of security for the reelection committee. Everyone in the White House was expected to devote his energies to getting Nixon reelected, no matter what his regularly assigned role was. From the beginning, it was understood that any method necessary was to be employed to keep Nixon in office.

Liddy's presence was clear testimony to that fact. The former FBI man was unpredictable and unstable. For instance, as the campaign began, Liddy showed up in presidential counsel John Dean's office sporting a bandaged hand. Dean asked Liddy about the injury, and Liddy remarked offhandedly that he had to show some men that he was a man of strength so he held his hand over a candle until the flesh burned.[2] After the Watergate burglary, Liddy bragged that he had shown his manliness another time by biting the head off a rat. The reelection effort was out of control.

Still, the election would be decided not by CREEP's mistakes, but by the miscues and weaknesses in the Democratic field. Among the Democrats were 1968 presidential nominee and former Vice President Hubert Humphrey; Humphrey's running mate, Edmund Muskie, a senator from Maine; George Wallace, governor of Alabama, who had been an independent presidential candidate in 1968; South Dakota Senator George McGovern; Washington Senator Henry Jackson; and New York Mayor John Lindsay, who had just switched parties. Senator Edward Kennedy of Massachusetts had announced after the Chappaquiddick incident in 1969 that he would not be a candidate in 1972, though until the nominating process was completed, Nixon and his staff did not believe Kennedy's noncandidacy.

Each declared Democrat carried heavy baggage. Humphrey had lost the nomination in 1960 and the general election in 1968. He had served as Lyndon Johnson's vice president, and the left found his close association with the Vietnam War unacceptable. Voters felt Humphrey's time had come and gone. Jackson was too conservative and stodgy for young, left-wing voters. McGovern was generally unknown, except for his attempt to substitute his name for Robert F. Kennedy's at the 1968 convention, and he was too liberal. Wallace was seen as a racist and a third-party turncoat by a large percentage of the Democrats. Lindsay had just changed parties, making his Democratic credentials suspect. Only Muskie seemed to be untainted, and he was the prohibitive favorite as the campaign opened in New Hampshire.

In a telephone conversation in September 1971, speechwriter Patrick Buchanan told Nixon to exaggerate Muskie's position on school busing to anger voters in the South. "Except the thing to do really is to praise him, have some civil rights people praise him for his defense of busing," Nixon responded. "That's the way to really get that, you know. It's much the better way than to have people attack him for it—is to praise him for his defense of busing, see? And I don't [know] if you've got any people to do that or not. But I would think that would be very clever."[3] It was obvious that Nixon, who publicly supported the concept of integration, saw busing as a means to aggravate race relations in the United States, if it served his political purposes. Later, he would call "a moratorium" on busing to gain votes.

During an antiwar demonstration in Washington, D.C., in May 1971, Nixon operatives sent a crate of oranges to some of the jailed demonstrators. Muskie had a habit of sending oranges to friends and it was hoped that the public would make a connection among Muskie, the demonstrators, and the oranges. The decision to send the oranges arose from a joking discussion in the White House among John Ehrlichman, Dean, Dean's assistant Fred Fielding, and Nixon aide Charles Colson. Colson took the idea seriously and immediately rushed out to order the oranges, but none of the media seemed to associate the fruit with the Muskie campaign.[4]

In August 1971, Haldeman aide Gordon Strachan advised Haldeman that he had ideas for "political intelligence and covert activities." Dwight Chapin, an aide to Buchanan, recruited California lawyer Donald Segretti to begin a dirty tricks campaign.[5] A spy was planted in the Muskie campaign, apparently a chauffeur. Another Nixon operative rose to a position of influence in Humphrey's Philadelphia headquarters. In an Oval Office conversation in January 1973, Colson confirmed that CREEP had planted listening devices in McGovern's headquarters and in the offices of Gary Hart, McGovern's campaign chair.[6] Nixon staffers spent $10,000 to sponsor a campaign in California to keep Wallace off the ballot there.[7] Haldeman approved at that time a hefty increase in spending for subversive campaign tactics. Soon bagmen were carrying around briefcases stuffed with cash, as much as a million dollars, to hire operatives to sabotage Democratic campaigns. Segretti crisscrossed the country planning for and spending money on covert activities.[8]

The Nixon staff used traditional ways to undercut Muskie, too. In February 1972, Muskie told a group of churchwomen in New Hampshire that the president was mishandling the Vietnam War. At Nixon's insistence, Haldeman called in presidential aide Charles Colson and press officer John Scali to discuss rebuttal tactics. Secretary of State William Rogers was asked to respond in kind to Muskie, which he did, accusing Muskie of sabotaging the peace talks. This created a stir and brought a fairly negative attack on Rogers by *New York Times* columnist James R. "Scotty" Reston. Haldeman noted in his diary that the White House was able to get columnist Stewart Alsop to criticize Muskie in *Newsweek*, but generally Muskie suffered in the polls.[9]

While the latter episode is not as underhanded or as shocking as some of the other Nixon tactics, it reveals how the Nixon White House functioned. Legitimate cabinet officers, supposedly directing the nation's business, were used as political puppets. It is interesting that neither Press Secretary Ronald Ziegler nor Communications Director Herbert Klein was consulted or asked to plan strategy when Haldeman organized the press response to Muskie. Nixon sent Haldeman a memo, and Haldeman issued orders as to what was to be done, circumventing the official White House press apparatus. When serious communications strategy was employed using whatever tactics were necessary, the orders nearly always came from Nixon through Haldeman, a point that will be expanded in the discussions of the planning of dirty tricks, including the Watergate break-in. Rogers's comments about Muskie also show how the Nixon people still manipulated columnists and reporters as late as 1972, though most of the press hardly dealt with the White House inner circle by that time. Nixon and Haldeman kept lists of "favorable" and "unfavorable" reporters so that stories could be planted and journalists influenced, especially around reelection time. The Nixon White House had been planning strategy for the win-at-all-costs 1972 campaign essentially as soon as Nixon took office. Lists, wiretaps, and surveillance from as early as 1969 were groundwork for making certain that Nixon stayed in the White House for eight years.

HALDEMAN INTERVIEW

In an unusual move in February 1972, Haldeman granted a rare two-hour interview to NBC's Barbara Walters for the *Today* show. Haldeman lashed out at Muskie, calling his comments almost "treasonous." Because many viewers were seeing and hearing Haldeman for the first time—he hardly ever gave interviews and preferred to work behind the scenes—Haldeman purposely exaggerated his criticism, hoping that his unusual television appearance combined with the strong remarks would have the greatest effect. Haldeman later rarely addressed the issue of the surreptitious campaign activities. Haldeman's published diary mentions only the public quarrels with the press and Muskie. The dirty tricks campaign organized by Haldeman, Ehrlichman, and Colson is never discussed.

In the spring of 1972, Nixon tried to short-circuit George Wallace's campaign by again playing politics with school busing for integration. Knowing that busing had become a hot issue in both the North and South, Nixon announced on March 16 that he was ordering a moratorium. Courts could not issue edicts for any new busing to achieve racial integration during the moratorium. He also called upon Congress to allocate $2.5 billion to help achieve integration in schools without busing. The two measures were impossible to implement, but it was hoped that such comments would split support on the right between Wallace and Nixon.

But the underhanded approach, not the political maneuvering, was the one that the White House favored in 1972. That same month, Colson's office created a letter and distributed it publicly. It contained what was purported to be offhand remarks by Muskie using an epithet about French Canadians ("Canucks") and laughing at a description of French Canadians as New Hampshire blacks. In his memoirs, Colson denied having any knowledge of the letter, but he noted that others had claimed that it was written by one of his aides, Kenneth Clawson, who had previously worked as a reporter for the *Washington Post*. Colson pointedly does not deny that Clawson wrote the letter, only that he, Colson, did not know about it at the time.[10] The "Canuck" letter and attacks on Muskie's wife, Jane, by the right-wing *Manchester News Leader*, owned by William Loeb, incensed the Democratic front-runner. On a snowy day in late February a pickup truck stopped in front of the newspaper offices in Manchester. Muskie climbed onto the bed of the truck and denounced Loeb as a "gutless coward," He broke down in tears. Muskie's huge lead in New Hampshire disappeared and he barely beat McGovern with 46.4 percent of the vote to McGovern's 37.2 percent. Muskie won Illinois but finished fourth in Florida and Wisconsin, and his campaign was over within two months of his tearful outburst. The Nixon dirty tricks strategy had contributed to the downfall of Nixon's most serious opponent.

But that was not enough. Liddy had other plans. He wanted to spend a million dollars to sabotage the Democratic National Convention in Miami in July by shutting down the air conditioning.[11] Liddy was paid $250,000 in December 1971 to work on a plan to vandalize the convention, according to testimony from deputy CREEP director Jeb Stuart Magruder. Magruder told an FBI agent in March 1973 that he was shocked to learn that Liddy had spent nearly all the $250,000 within a few months and that CREEP Finance Committee treasurer Hugh Sloan was not asking Liddy for receipts.[12] Sloan apparently was suggesting that Liddy may have used the money to plan and execute the Watergate burglary on his own, an explanation that would conveniently exculpate all others on the CREEP staff. At any rate, Liddy's wild schemes were beginning to worry the White House.

Underhanded strategy flowed from the top in many cases. In April Nixon told Haldeman that a good way to undercut the apparent Democratic nominee, McGovern, was to issue false polls, touting McGovern as doing well in trial heats. This would build momentum for McGovern over Humphrey (Nixon correctly saw McGovern as the weakest of his potential opponents) and would help Nixon when real polls later in the year showed Nixon far ahead, indicating that the president had made an amazing comeback.[13]

There were other childish or deceitful tactics used but rarely discussed during the Watergate investigations. Pizzas were ordered and sent to some Democratic candidates' headquarters by CREEP operatives. Confused Democratic staffers were left to argue about payment for the pizzas. Sometimes unpopular groups were paid to endorse Democrats. According to an FBI interview with Magruder, CREEP paid $30,000 to a group called Peace and Freedom to put out a pamphlet, *Why a Liberal Should Vote for McGovern*. Magruder told the FBI agent that he received the money from Sloan and from Herbert L. Porter, CREEP's scheduling director. By spending the money, the CREEP people figured they were tying McGovern to an ultraliberal group abhorred by the mainstream public. The group, in return, apparently abandoned its principles to accept the cash.[14]

There is a hint of press scandal in that FBI report. A well-respected columnist traditionally friendly with Nixon was paid an unspecified sum in cash and cashier's checks over the 1972 campaign apparently to write favorably about Nixon and unfavorably about McGovern, Magruder told Special Agent Angelo J Lano. The columnist's name is spelled incorrectly in the FBI report and the information is unsubstantiated, so this author has chosen not to use his name here, but at one point Magruder told Lano that both Sloan and Fred LaRue (another CREEP officer) were present when the columnist was paid some of the money. Magruder said the money came from cash stored in a safe "in Porter's possession." In the same report, Magruder clearly indicated that other reporters were on the Nixon payroll. Agent Lano wrote in his report: "He [Magruder] stated that this latter form [cashier's checks] was always used by the news media because that was the way they requested it be handled [paid]."[15]

If Magruder's allegations are correct, the results of the 1972 election and the reasons that reporters so long ignored Watergate might be connected. How many reporters did CREEP pay off, and who were they? Were key correspondents cowed by the Nixon White House or just paid off? It seems likely that the payments were not widespread, and it is certain that McGovern would have lost badly anyway, but the 1973 memo opens many questions about editorial columnists and White House correspondents in the early 1970s and adds one facet to a sad tale of corruption in the 1972 election.

But even without the help of CREEP, the Democrats experienced a series of setbacks in 1972. Kennedy had decided not to run and Muskie had been eliminated as a force in the 1972 campaign, but George Wallace suffered an even more devastating blow. On May 15, while campaigning in Maryland, Wallace was shot by a Milwaukee man, Arthur Bremer. The former Alabama governor barely survived, was wheelchair-bound for the rest of his life, and could not campaign actively for the presidency. That ended his hopes in 1972 and thereafter. Wallace had won the Florida and Michigan primaries (he also won in Maryland even after being shot), and it was anticipated before the shooting that the Democrats would have to make concessions to Wallace at the convention or face another of his independent campaigns.

Only McGovern and Humphrey remained viable candidates by late spring. Then McGovern won the California primary in June to sew up the nomination. The Nixon White House was preoccupied with other matters, and McGovern's triumph gave them little comfort. Within days of McGovern's triumph, the *Washington Post* uncovered the story of the Watergate break-in and its possible connections to the White House. While publicly seeking reelection, Nixon spent most of his time during the summer of 1972 with his inner circle, trying to figure out how to cover up the White House's involvement in a series of dirty tricks, including the burglary.

Significantly, FBI Director J. Edgar Hoover, died on May 2, 1972. Hoover had been director for more than forty years. No president had the courage to fire him, because he kept private dossiers on everyone in power, including presidents. Nixon had made the decision to fire Hoover months earlier, but when he met with the FBI chief, the president could not go through with it. After Hoover's death, Nixon named L. Patrick Gray the interim director. Just as the general election campaign was beginning and as the Watergate burglary details unfolded, the FBI was in an unsettled state with a new director for the first time since the Great Depression.

Although the underhanded tactics went largely undetected by the press corps, reporters did not trust the Nixon people. While the Watergate investigation was left largely to the *Washington Post* for a variety of reasons (see Chapter 5), the media still found much to question about the reelection campaign and pursued irregularities when they surfaced. Mitchell appeared on CBS's *Face the Nation* panel interview show on June 11, 1972, six days before the Watergate break-in. His inquisitors were George Herman and Dan Rather of CBS and Peter Lisagor, Washington bureau chief of the *Chicago Daily News*. Herman asked why Mitchell had not disclosed the sources of the ten million dollars that CREEP had collected. Mitchell said that it was not necessary, that it might embarrass some of the ninety thousand to one hundred thousand contributors, and that "there is no possibility of anybody contributing to the re-election of the president having any influence in the administration of this government so long as Richard Nixon is in office." The real reason was that much of the money had been contributed illegally and that millions of dollars were being spent on dirty tricks. At the very least, the panelists found the lack of disclosure odd and apparently sensed something wrong in the way the campaign was being run. About half the interview was spent on the topic of the lack of disclosure. Rather also asked Mitchell why Buchanan told reporters that "if the press doesn't change that there could be pressure from citizens and possibly antitrust legislation." (Indeed, the Nixon administration did have plans in late 1972 to attack opposition media through antitrust cases, but it decided against pursuing that approach.) Mitchell simply disavowed Buchanan's remarks, but the panel had raised questions about ominous portents within the Nixon administration, even before the Watergate break-in.[16]

McGovern's nomination was a disaster for the Democratic Party. Not only was he relatively unknown, despite his two-year campaign for the nomination (the longest in history to that point), but he was a dovish, left-wing liberal whose voter base had begun to dissipate as the Vietnam War wound down. The anger of 1968, 1969, and 1970 had been replaced by an indifference to Southeast Asia. The world had moved on.

CONVENTION DEBACLE

The July Miami convention was not what the Democrats had hoped for. After the 1968 debacle in Chicago, the rules had changed. All discussion was to be undertaken in public, and minorities and women were to be amply represented. Delegations were to reflect a politically correct balance. Traditional Democrats, including Mayor Richard Daley of Chicago and his contingent, were left out of the convention. In return, when the general election campaign was underway, Daley and his people sat on their hands, as did many traditional party supporters.

The platform included planks for peace and a cut in military expenditures, abolition of capital punishment, a ban on handguns, reform of Congress, redistribution of wealth through changes in tax codes, and direct election of presidents. These highly principled and idealistic liberal measures moved the party too far to the left for most voters. Party platforms, though usually controversial, historically had been hammered out in private with compromises that neither wing of the party particular liked but accepted as a price for unity. In Miami, the fight was public and there were few compromises. Many factions were alienated from a political party that was losing public support anyway. The election that seemed to threaten the incumbent only a year earlier was turning into a fiasco.

On Thursday, the last day of the convention, McGovern named Senator Thomas Eagleton as his vice presidential nominee. Because this was an open convention, others stepped forward on Thursday night to nominate alternative names. The debate over the vice presidential nomination and over procedural matters lasted into the early morning hours. McGovern did not deliver his acceptance speech until 3 A.M., long after viewers had gone to bed. Practically no one heard his oratory.

The Republican convention in late August was also in Miami, but there were no problems with the nominating procedures or the credentials of the delegates. Nixon's people spent lavishly to make certain that everything proceeded without error. Nixon antagonist Nelson Rockefeller nominated the president for reelection. Arizona Senator Barry Goldwater, the 1964 standard-bearer, made a supportive speech, as did California Governor Ronald Reagan. Elements of the party from both left and right stood behind Nixon. The only suspense in August was about Nixon's decision to rename Spiro Agnew to the ticket, which he did before the convention. The difference to viewers between the Democratic and Republican conventions was stark. Conventions usually don't matter in modern times, but the Democrats did their best to shoot themselves in the feet in Miami. The Democrats were disorganized and contentious; the Republicans were organized and harmonious.

Miami was only the beginning. While Nixon operatives plotted their way through the summer of 1972, McGovern and his staff gave the president all the help he needed without the dirty tricks. Just after McGovern's nomination, reporters from Knight Newspapers and *Time* magazine were on the trail of a story about Eagleton. The vice presidential nominee had been hospitalized in 1960, 1964, and 1966 for emotional problems. Twice he had received electroshock treatments in hospitals in St. Louis and Minnesota. At the time, he told reporters that he was suffering from stomach disorders. To reduce the influence of the potential stories, McGovern and Eagleton held a press conference three days after the convention and released the details of Eagleton's hospitalizations. They hoped that would end the matter, and they both set off to campaign. Americans were unable to deal with the concept of a vice president with mental health problems, however. It was still an era when little was publicly understood about mental health disorders and their treatment.

McGovern could not escape the questions. No reporter seemed interested in the issues McGovern wanted to talk about. Campaign contributions dried up. Ten days after he was named to the ticket, Eagleton withdrew. McGovern offered the nomination to just about everyone he could think of—Edward Kennedy, Muskie, Humphrey, Senator Abraham Ribicoff, Democratic Party Chairman Lawrence O'Brien, Florida Governor Reuben Askew—and finally to Sargent Shriver, a Kennedy in-law and former Peace Corps director, who accepted.

McGovern entered the campaign as a heavy underdog. The mistakes of the summer simply ensured that the election would be a landslide. Polls indicated that only 6 percent of the public thought Nixon had anything to do with Watergate, but they all heard and saw McGovern's mistakes. McGovern was seen as a dangerously unrealistic radical whose party was so out of control that its candidate could not deliver his acceptance speech at a reasonable hour and as a party leader who had to recant his own vice presidential nominee just days after he had made the most important decision of his short presidential candidacy. If George McGovern could not keep his own house in order, then who could trust him to negotiate with the Russians, handle relations with the Chinese, keep stability in the Middle East, end the war honorably, oversee busing for integration, steady the economy, provide a reasonable social safety net, and keep a lid on federal spending? Big Labor had abandoned him, urban political bosses were offended by his remarks and the convention snubs, and mainstream America saw him as a dangerous radical.

Nixon played upon people's fears. Republican campaign advertising depicted McGovern as antilabor, suggesting that he would make half the country eligible for welfare, if he were elected. His vote for the Gulf of Tonkin Resolution in 1964 providing for an escalation of the Vietnam War was compared with his 1972 stance opposing the war, suggesting that McGovern could never make up his mind. Of course, McGovern and nearly all his colleagues voted for the Gulf of Tonkin Resolution before it was known what the impact of the war might be. Many changed their minds in the late 1960s, and he never advocated a plan that would place half the country on public aid. But the ads were effective. Voters believed them.

McGovern's campaign staff tried to play up Nixon's role in Watergate and to link Nixon with illegal campaign activity, but voters did not believe that. It was too outrageous to be logical. Even reporters found the allegations that Nixon was tied to Watergate a difficult leap. No one could be that stupid and clumsy, the reasoning went; there had to be another explanation.

Twenty-first-century students of history wonder how it was that Richard Nixon could have won so easily in 1972 when his White House had so brazenly broken the law and the facts were becoming known. What were voters thinking? Couldn't they have seen the truth? The answer was: not yet. Voters wanted to believe in Nixon. He was within a few months of ending the longest war in American history, the last major U.S. war of the twentieth century—the bloodiest century in history. He had opened the door to China, and he had kept a decaying economy under control. In the fall of 1972, consumer prices had risen only 2.9 percent during the previous twelve months and wholesale farm prices were up 4.3 percent, but hourly earnings had increased by 5.7 percent and unemployment had dropped from 6.0 percent to 5.5 percent. Real weekly spendable earnings were up 4 percent, and total civilian employment was up by 2.4 million jobs, the largest twelve-month increase in postwar America. The unemployment figure was about average for the 1960s and early 1970s. It had been as low as 3.5 percent in 1969 but as high as 6.7 percent in 1961. The American domination of the world economy from 1947 to 1973 was about to end, but not in 1972.[17]

Additionally, the 1960s had been a decade of transition and controversy. Assassinations, war, and the generation gap had bewildered many Americans. They yearned for more normal times, and Nixon, an old familiar face, seemed to deliver. Besides holding the line on the economy, Nixon had said he would end the war and he was about to. He said he would speak for the silent majority and he seemed to. He stood up to the Eastern Establishment and to the reporters in Washington, who seemed preoccupied with criticizing America and what it stood for and with tearing down everything that the World War II generation had built.

McGovern, on the other hand, appeared to promise nothing but more turmoil and anxiety. If the convention and the appointment of Eagleton proved nothing else, they showed that McGovern would never bring back stability. McGovern seemed to voters to be not only incompetent, but also the wrong candidate at the wrong time. The anger of the 1960s had dissolved and in its wake was simple uncertainty. McGovern not only made mistakes, but he also sought office four years too late. The world had changed.

The *New York Times* endorsed McGovern early, but few other newspapers did. Nixon drew three times as many newspaper endorsements, but few of them from the East Coast. About 30 percent of newspapers chose not to endorse either candidate, a high percentage for the 1970s, though that number would become commonplace in later decades.

Reporters found it difficult to develop original campaign stories. They all pointed to the same theme: a one-sided Nixon victory. McGovern and his staff granted interviews to reporters and shared ideas and thoughts with them as often as possible. Nixon hardly had any contact with the press. The Nixon campaign hired advance people to make certain that cheering audiences carrying supportive signs were at every Nixon stop. The "Nixon girls," wearing bathing suits and straw hats, danced at Nixon festivities. The president smiled and waved a great deal, imploring Americans to remember the men who died in Vietnam and the man who had led them from the war.

So, although the Watergate break-in story was over a month old, the Nixon campaign was still unstoppable. The Nixon camp ignored McGovern and refused to accept an offer for debates. After the historic 1960 Nixon-Kennedy confrontations, Americans experienced their third presidential election in a row without a televised match of ideas. This campaign was the last without a debate. There were three in 1976 and more than one debate every four years thereafter. But in 1972, there were only question-and-answer sessions between Nixon and his handpicked audiences. Nixon never participated in another debate after he lost the presidency in 1960.

ELECTION NIGHT

The mood was grim in the McGovern headquarters on election night. The distraught candidate had simply said whatever he wanted to as the campaign ended. He told one heckler, "Kiss my ass." There was nothing left for him to do in the last week, but plug along gamely and take his medicine. At 10 P.M. Eastern Standard Time on election night, NBC anchor John Chancellor told his audience that Nixon would win "the most spectacular landslide in the history of U.S. politics. It may be the largest margin in history." Election chronicler Theodore White said on CBS that Nixon had discovered the working-class culture and that he knew how to talk to the blue-collar group in a way that McGovern was never able to. White also said that McGovern was for continuing the experiment of the 1960s, but that people were tired of being the subjects of experimentation.[18]

Voter turnout was light, only 55.2 percent, the lowest presidential year turnout in twenty-four years. That was a continuing trend after the 1960 election, when one of the most exciting campaigns of the twentieth century brought out 62.8 percent. On election night 1972, Nixon collected every electoral vote except those from Massachusetts and the District of Columbia, winning the Electoral College 520 to 17. He had 218 more electoral votes than in 1968. His popular vote of 47,165,234 (60.7 percent) to McGovern's 29,170,774 (38.9 percent) was not only the largest presidential candidate total up to that time, but it also provided the largest numerical margin of victory and the largest number of states for one candidate (49). He became the first Republican president to carry every state in the South. In many cases, he not only carried the Southern states, but also annihilated McGovern there. Mississippi cast 78 percent of its vote for Nixon, Georgia 75 percent, Alabama 73 percent, Florida 72 percent, South Carolina 71 percent, Arkansas 69 percent, and Virginia 68 percent. Just a generation earlier, those numbers had been reversed. The South had stampeded to the Republican standard-bearer.

But not to the Republicans. The congressional elections suggest that the key to explaining the 1972 presidential election was that it was not a Republican endorsement, but a McGovern repudiation. In the Senate the Republicans lost two seats, increasing the Democrats' total to fifty-seven compared with forty-three for the Republicans. In the House, the GOP gained twelve seats, but still trailed badly, 243 to 192. Clearly, the Republicans had not captured the hearts and minds of voters. Never had such a landslide been accompanied by such short coattails.

It would be simple just to blame McGovern's incompetence and blundering campaign. Certainly, he deserves much of the fault, but major elections defy simplistic explanations. Many factors contributed to the landslide, not the least of which was that the White House had kept a lid on the Watergate investigation. Watergate was not a major ingredient in the campaign of 1972.

Explaining what did happen, not just what didn't, is important, too. Despite his repeated claims of persecution from the press, Nixon was treated very well in the coverage of the 1972 campaign. Not only did he receive the majority of newspaper endorsements, but also most of the coverage emphasized McGovern's shortcomings and Nixon's accomplishments. Nixon buried McGovern with a public relations and press control blitz. The president had learned how to create an image better than any other politician in the country.

At the same time, the public Nixon represented what Americans wanted in 1972, not only the stability mentioned earlier, but also the strength of leadership shown in China and in domestic policy decisions and the conservatism of Republican presidential leadership. It appeared in November 1972 that Richard Nixon would help Americans return to the tranquility of the 1950s. Voters rewarded Nixon for giving them what they had sought for a decade: a way out of the turmoil.

That is why Watergate so devastated America. It came right on the heels of Vietnam and at a time when voters had overwhelmingly placed their faith in one man. Nixon allowed them to hope that the White House was still a citadel of respectability and moral leadership. Fifty-eight-thousand Americans had died in the war in Vietnam and soon it would be over. Americans wanted to know that it all meant something and that what they had read in the Pentagon Papers about the lies and covert planning had all been put behind. Now there was a president with four more years of leadership ahead of him, most of which could be spent on matters other than war. Voters had elected an image they fervently wanted to believe in. When that image was destroyed—when Americans came to believe that Nixon did not really represent what they had voted for—there was trouble for the White House, and the presidency would never be quite the same again.

The election victory was met with mixed feelings inside the West Wing. The Nixon staff rejoiced in the trouncing of McGovern, but those around Nixon knew that they had to continue to act forcefully to prevent the Watergate mess from undercutting their victory. To that end, they had to hush up the staff even more than in the first four years.

Immediately after the election, Haldeman asked for the resignations of everyone in the White House. The purpose was to make it clear that, despite all the hard work and success, no one's job was safe. Most were rehired, but the point was made. With the second term safely assured, Nixon, Haldeman, and Ehrlichman would pursue Nixon's agenda without any restraint. No one was to get in the way, particularly reporters.

Days after the election, a general White House memo advised staff members that they should familiarize themselves with White House rules regarding their personal papers and communications, "particularly if you expect to leave the staff." All papers had to be sent to "Central Files" before anyone left the employ of the White House. Those papers would later be transferred to the future presidential library. "All other members of the staff should inventory and review their files of official business which are inactive and no longer needed. These files will be stored by office, as well as listed by subject matter and will be readily available for your future reference. . . . compliance with these procedures will be an expression of loyalty by you to the President."[19] The message was clear: fidelity and silence were required for the next four years.

In December 1972 Haldeman and Ehrlichman combined Klein's and Ziegler's offices, giving Ziegler a stronger, yet still not influential, role in the White House. Klein stayed until June 1973. Just after the election he set up a photograph of Nixon in the Oval Office with Henry O. Dormann, publisher and chairman of the board of the *National Enquirer*, the scandalous newspaper that drew heavy readership with defamatory stories, usually fictitious, about the private lives of movie stars and other public figures. In his memo to Nixon, Klein said that the photo was a good idea because of Dormann's support for Nixon in the election and because Dormann had taken the newspaper from "gossip sheet status to its highly respectable position today as the nation's largest weekly publication with over three million circulation.[20] Klein never did quite get it.

The concept of split press responsibilities would be revived under Ronald Reagan, a decade later. Although Ziegler was the only major press officer (in name) for the remaining twenty months of the Nixon administration, Nixon had greatly influenced the role of the press secretary.

The main objective as 1972 ended was to get past Watergate and move toward building Nixon's place in history. Bob Woodward's and Carl Bernstein's lead role was ending as a District of Columbia grand jury session opened and the Senate Watergate Committee inquiry waited in the wings. The taping system kept recording conversations into July 1973, and that would be the key to reversing the overwhelming results of the tainted 1972 election. Many twists and turns would take place from June 1972 to July 1973 before the results of the 1972 election came unraveled.

NOTES

1. H. R. Haldeman, *The Haldeman Diaries: Inside the White House* (New York: G. P. Putnam's Sons 1994), September 19, 1971, entry, 356–57.

2. John Dean, *Blind Ambition: The White House Years* (New York: Simon and Schuster, 1976), 78–79.

3. Nixon and Patrick Buchanan, White House telephone conversation, September 22, 1971, White House Tapes.

4. Dean, *Blind Ambition*, 43.

5. Ibid., 72.

6. Oval Office conversation between Nixon and Charles Colson, January 8, 1973, Exhibit 5 tape, *U.S. vs. Mitchell et al.* (original Watergate tapes used in prosecuting Watergate figures in 1973 and 1974), p. 1.

7. Theodore White, *Breach of Faith: The Fall of Richard Nixon* (New York: Atheneum, 1975), 154–55.

8. Dean, *Blind Ambition*, 72–73.

9. H. R. Haldeman, *The Haldeman Diaries*, February 3, 1972, and February 4, 1972, entries, 406.

10. Charles W. Colson, *Born Again* (Old Tappan, N.J.: Chosen Books, 1976), 65.

11. Dean, *Blind Ambition*, 84–85.

12. FBI Special Agent Angelo J. Lano, report of interview with Jeb Stuart Magruder, March 14, 1973, p. 3, University of Illinois Library Nixon-Watergate microfilm collection, Urbana, Illinois.

13. Haldeman, *The Haldeman Diaries*, April 29, 1972, entry, 449.

14. Jeb Magruder, interview with FBI Special Agent Lano, 2.

15. Ibid., 1–2.

16. Transcript of *Face the Nation* broadcast, June 11, 1972, Ziegler Papers, Box 18, 1–4, 11.

17. Herbert Stein, memo to Nixon about the economy in preparation for the October 9, 1972, Quadriad Meeting, October 6, 1972, and Press Memo on Employment Rate in civilian workforce, November 1972, both in Ziegler Papers, Box 6, miscellaneous file.

18. White House News Summary of "Election Night Coverage," November 7–8, 1972, 1–3, Ziegler Papers, Box 3, Election Returns (1972) file.

19. White House memorandum, "Presidential Papers," undated from November 1972 files, Ziegler Papers, Box 4, Government Reorganization files.

20. Herbert G. Klein to Nixon, memo, December 4, 1972, Ziegler Papers, Box 6, miscellaneous file, 2.

Chapter 5

A Cancer on the Presidency

Richard Nixon's landslide victory over George McGovern came to be one of the most conflicted triumphs in U.S. political history. While Nixon was burying McGovern publicly, he was entombing his presidency privately. The events of the immediate post-Watergate era are seen differently a generation later because of the release of the Abuse of Government Power tapes. While the chain of events that ensued after the break-in are perhaps some of the most widely discussed in the history of the presidency, the taped conversations provide a much different spin on the Nixon inner circle's culpability.

There are also a number of retrospective questions that have been addressed only superficially and that bear discussion here. Some examples: Who ordered the Watergate break-in, and who knew what when? Was a formal press strategy developed within the White House inner circle to lead reporters away from the Watergate-related dirty tricks campaign, thus explaining why only the *Washington Post* was interested in the story? Also, this chapter will provide a wide sample of newspaper and news magazine press coverage for the period of June 18 to December 31, 1972, to illustrate just how well the print media covered Watergate before, during, and just after the 1972 general election campaign, and to discover whether leading newspapers and magazines really did ignore Watergate.

As to the first question about the person behind the burglary: Nixon always claimed that he had no prior knowledge of Watergate. In his memoirs he asserted that the first he knew of the break-in was when he read a small article on the front page of the *Miami Herald* on Sunday, June 18, 1972, while he was vacationing with his friend Bebe Rebozo in Key Biscayne, Florida. He wrote that he spoke with Chief of Staff H. R. Haldeman on Saturday, the day the burglars were arrested (June 17), but they did not discuss the incident. After reading the article, he spoke by telephone with Haldeman, aide Charles Colson, his two daughters and wife Pat (none of his family was vacationing with him), Treasury Secretary John Connally, National Security Advisor Henry Kissinger, and Deputy National Security Advisor Alexander Haig. Nixon claimed not to have discussed the burglary with any of them on Sunday either. He maintained that he learned about the connection with CREEP on Monday, June 19, when Haldeman called and informed him of the relationship. Haldeman obtained his information from CREEP Chairman John Mitchell, who had said that one of the burglars, James McCord, was a former CIA officer who was working for CREEP.[1]

John Ehrlichman, presidential advisor for domestic affairs, claimed not to have known about the burglary beforehand either, though he admitted to having known about the break-in at psychiatrist Lewis Fielding's office in September 1971 just hours after it occurred. Ehrlichman alleged that his only mistake about Watergate was not urging Nixon to come clean immediately, and he said that Colson knew more than anyone.[2] John Dean, in a conversation with Nixon in the Oval Office on March 21, 1973, told the president that "a cancer was growing on the presidency." He suggested that it may have been Haldeman aide Gordon Strachan who ordered the break-in. Strachan was pushing for illicit information, and Jeb Magruder, deputy CREEP director, ordered G. Gordon Liddy (the burglary organizer) to get some information without saying specifically how, according to Dean.[3] Magruder said at a public seminar in 1987 that he told Liddy to return to the Democratic National Committee (DNC) headquarters on June 17 after consulting with Haldeman and Mitchell.

Haldeman argued in his memoirs that it was probably Nixon who told Colson to order the break-in. Haldeman also claimed that the CIA knew about the pending break-in before it occurred, because Eugenio Martinez, one of the burglars, was still working for the CIA.[4] In an addendum to his diary, Haldeman argued that there was not a cover-up in the days after the break-in, but just spin control to "contain, or minimize, any potential political damage."[5] Colson claimed not to have known about the break-in beforehand, and he wrote later that no one, including Nixon, "would for a moment tolerate or cover up such bungling incompetence. This was not a moral judgment on my part; the burglary seemed too stupid by the standards we set." Colson also claimed that when Nixon learned of the burglary, he was so angry he threw an ashtray across the room, denouncing the witlessness of the entire affair.[6] Thanks to the tapes, we know that many persons participated in the cover-up, including Nixon, Haldeman, Ehrlichman, and Colson.

In the FBI interview in March 1973, Magruder told the agent that he had authorized that Liddy be given $250,000 to disrupt the Democratic National Convention in Miami in July by sabotaging the air conditioning system (see Chapter 4). Magruder said he never knew what became of that money, implying that perhaps Liddy had gone off on his own and planned the Watergate burglary, using the $250,000 for the operation, contrary to what Magruder said in 1987.[7]

The author has dragged the reader through all these circular explanations to illustrate how difficult it is to assess the truth of anything pertaining to the Watergate investigation, especially the ordering of the burglary. Fingers pointed in every direction afterward, while no one disclosed the complete truth. As has been demonstrated, the Watergate break-in was only one in a series of clumsy but devious efforts to undercut the Democrats in 1971 and 1972. So much money was floating around and so many people were plotting campaign dirty tricks that it is not surprising, at first glance, that specific details about this one action would be easily forgotten by the White House.

But one fact has been forgotten in this first analysis. This was not the first break-in at the Democratic National Committee headquarters in the Watergate complex. The burglars were fixing eavesdropping devices that had not been working, while installing others. The original break-in had occurred three weeks earlier on May 27.

It seems likely that after the first breach of the offices, someone would have reported the results to the White House inner circle. At the very least, it is likely that Liddy would have bragged to his superiors about how the devices were inside the offices and how the Nixon people could now listen to what was being said by the leaders of the opposition party. Why would they plant the bugs and then tell no one in the campaign that they could hear everything said inside the offices of their party opponents? If Liddy had told Magruder, Colson, or Strachan, would the message have stopped there? Would any of those three really have kept to himself the knowledge that there were listening devices in the DNC offices and not told Haldeman or Ehrlichman? It seems unlikely, especially in view of how much minutiae flowed directly to Nixon through Haldeman during Nixon's first term in office. It may be that the planning of the original break-in was unknown or the details were not specifically given to Haldeman or Nixon, but certainly the president and his chief of staff would have known that the first listening devices were planted and would have authorized the second break-in on June 17.

Haldeman wrote specifically that he thought Nixon himself had ordered the break-in without Haldeman's knowledge. But White House operations didn't work that way. Nixon always told Haldeman to take care of details. He would not have bypassed Haldeman on such an order, because there were many, many dirty tricks going on in 1972. Why bypass Haldeman on this specific one, especially when the Democratic National Committee was involved? Nixon simply would have told Haldeman to handle it. Haldeman's speculation about Nixon's culpability is an obvious attempt to draw attention away from himself. Later, the famous unidentified source, Deep Throat, told *Washington Post* reporter Bob Woodward that the entire series of dirty tricks and CREEP financing was a Haldeman operation. That seems the most logical explanation. The simplest explanation is usually the right one.

On Tuesday, June 20, 1972, after Nixon had flown back to the White House, the first recorded Watergate conversations took place. The infamous tape with an 18½-minute gap contained a discussion between Nixon and Haldeman in the Oval Office that morning. The tape was erased five or six times, according to electronics experts. In 2000, a taping specialist named Stephen St. Croix began trying to recover part of the missing 18½ minutes by using twenty-first century rejuvenation techniques. He had no luck at first. The tape's being erased at least five times destroys the argument presented during the Watergate investigation that Nixon's secretary, Rose Mary Woods, had accidentally deleted the conversation while transcribing it.

Someone had intentionally destroyed the recording. Why that particular one when there were many other "smoking gun" tapes? It must have been extremely incriminating. Because it was a conversation between Nixon and Haldeman, one can speculate that the tape likely shows that both Nixon and Haldeman had known of the burglary details beforehand and had authorized it. Or, less likely, it shows that they had specific plans to cover up the illegal act with more illegal acts (other tapes show that, so why destroy just this one?). Whatever is on that tape would have changed some perceptions, but in the long run it is only a minor curiosity. In the ensuing weeks and months, enough information came out to convict twenty-five Watergate figures and convince a congressional committee that Nixon had illegally participated in the cover-up of the break-in. In 1974 Nixon was pardoned. The erased tape would have added just a little more evidence of his and Haldeman's felonious acts.

Who was Bob Woodward's source, Deep Throat? Woodward, of course, was the reporter who was sitting in intake court the morning of June 17, 1972, when the Watergate burglars were brought in for their initial court appearances. He noticed that the five had rather high-priced lawyers. He and Carl Bernstein, another young *Post* reporter, followed the story for the remainder of the Watergate scandal. Their exploits in the unfolding exposé were chronicled in two books and a popular movie, and the *Post* earned two Pulitzer Prizes for Watergate reporting. Often, Woodward met in out-of-the-way places with a source his staff dubbed "Deep Throat," a title borrowed from a Linda Lovelace pornographic movie circulating at that time.

The identity of the source is really of no historical significance either, unless he was a major figure in the Nixon administration, but it is certainly a public curiosity. Persons who may have served as the shadowy source include an aide to John Dean, the president of a private company with CIA ties, a State Department underling, someone in the attorney general's office, Haig, Kissinger, or someone in the CIA. The person could be an obscure Nixon administration official with a penchant for intrigue or possibly no one at all, but someone Woodward made up. An investigative reporting class at the University of Illinois in 1999 and 2000, under the direction of former *Chicago Tribune* reporter Bill Gaines, attempted to use computer spreadsheets to identify the government officials who lived near Woodward and to narrow that list to who might have been Deep Throat (Woodward and Bernstein's book seemed to indicate that Deep Throat lived near Woodward). The group came up with the name of

Patrick Buchanan, a Nixon speechwriter and later a presidential candidate. They announced their findings on Dateline NBC during an episode that aired in June 2002, on the 30th anniversary of the break-in.

The identify of Deep Throat will remain a mystery until Deep Throat's death, Woodward has said. A generation later, Deep Throat must have been still alive. Because he came out of the Watergate scandal with his reputation intact, many suggest that it was Haig. Others argue that Haig was out of the country during times when Deep Throat allegedly was meeting with Woodward. Haig, however, seems the logical choice.

At any rate, events moved quickly. One of the burglary organizers, E. Howard Hunt, was arrested that weekend. Woodward learned that Hunt's name and the words, "White House" were in a notebook of one of the burglars. The Democratic National Committee immediately sued the Republican National Committee and CREEP for a million dollars. Press Secretary Ronald Ziegler, at a press briefing, declined to respond to questions about Watergate, saying it was "just a third-rate burglary." And contrary to what Nixon and his inner circle argued for years, the cover-up began as soon as Nixon returned to Washington. Ehrlichman placed White House counsel John Dean, who had joined Nixon's staff a year before, in charge of the cover-up.

In one of the worst assessments of talent in the history of the White House, during an Executive Office Building conversation on June 20 between Nixon and Haldeman, the chief of staff told the president that the five captured burglars were "a pretty competent bunch of people, and they've been doing other things well apparently." Haldeman also explained that James McCord (one of the burglars) was being paid a regular monthly retainer to gain information for the White House and that Hunt, who along with Gordon Liddy had organized the break-in, had disappeared. "He can undisappear if we want him to," Haldeman said. Nixon worried about the White House tapes, and Haldeman assured him that they were secure and that no one would learn of them. They decided that all the burglars would have to plead guilty to keep a lid on the investigation and that the FBI investigation would have to be blunted.[8] In conversations over the next few days, Nixon, Ehrlichman, and Haldeman reviewed how the press had reported on Watergate and seemed satisfied that they had controlled the public relations damage. They noted that most media were playing down the break-in. They also planned to continue to deny White House involvement.

CIA ORDERED TO BLOCK FBI

On June 23, Nixon and Haldeman met for an hour and a half. Haldeman advised Nixon that Dean and Mitchell were suggesting that CIA Director Richard Helms should be asked to tell FBI Acting Director L. Patrick Gray to "stay the hell out of this ... this is, ah, business here ... we don't want you to go any further on it." Gray's having replaced the deceased J. Edgar Hoover the month before placed the Bureau in a precarious position, although Gray refused to halt the investigation. Haldeman also revealed that $25,000 in hush money was being paid to Bernard Barker, one of the burglars, by a wealthy GOP contributor in Minnesota.[9] On June 26 Nixon and Haldeman decided that Mitchell had to resign as director of CREEP, and the long list of scapegoats in the scandal began.[10] Mitchell resigned a week later and was replaced by Clark MacGregor. Haldeman suggested on June 30 that the break-in be blamed entirely on Liddy, who was willing to take the fall.[11] Three weeks later, Nixon and Ehrlichman talked about having Deputy CREEP Director Jeb Magruder accept the blame for Watergate. "I hate to see it, but let me say we'll take care of Magruder immediately afterwards." Alluding to the case of Alger Hiss, the State Department official who Nixon pursued in 1948 until Hiss was convicted of perjury in a spy scandal, Nixon said prophetically to Ehrlichman, "If you cover up, you're going to get caught."[12]

Nixon admitted in his memoirs that he had ordered the CIA to blunt the FBI investigation just after the break-in. (He had no choice. The tape of that conversation had already been released.) He explained his actions this way: "I was handling in a pragmatic way what I perceived as an annoying and strictly political problem. I was looking for a way to deal with Watergate that would minimize the damage to me, my friends and my campaign, while giving the least advantage to my political opposition. I saw Watergate as politics pure and simple." He also claimed that the tapes released in 1974 distorted his thoughts and actions.[13] In fact, the tapes released in 1996 after his death prove that he was more devious than most had thought and that his only concern was to protect himself and sacrifice others.

The tapes indicate that, for the next several months, Nixon and his inner staff spent as much of their time covering up Watergate as worrying about the election or the press. There were five discussions about the *Washington Post* and how to pay it back, apparently because Woodward and Bernstein were aggressively pursuing the Watergate story. On August 9, while at Camp David, Nixon dictated a memorandum for Ehrlichman. Nixon had learned that columnist Joseph Alsop had told *Post* publisher Katherine Graham that the Nixon administration was going to challenge the license renewals of some of the *Post*-owned television stations in Florida. "You can point out that this administration has an impeccable record ... of never interfering with TV licenses. ... For your confidential information, [we will take care of] this whole matter of licenses after the election. [Let me know] what recommendations you have. Have this handled by one of your associates very discreetly. Don't talk to anyone else about it."[14] The Nixon staff also talked about challenging large media monopolies in antitrust cases after the election, but though some licenses were challenged, nothing adverse ever resulted in the courts or with the Federal Communications Commission. Nixon wanted a study about the "twenty most vicious Washington reporters and television people, and the title of this little memorandum would be 'Things That We'd Like To Forget They Said.'" Nixon wanted to plant articles in sympathetic newspapers about the twenty and what "predictions they have made with regard to the election. ... just kill the sons of bitches."[15] In an October 16 conversation, Nixon claimed that the *New York Times*, the *Washington Post*, and the *St. Louis Post-Dispatch*, the "Eastern establishment press," had been "strangely silent" about the "most libelous, slanderous, attack on the President in the history of American politics," referring to the McGovern campaign.[16] Actually, the press had been quite favorable to Nixon and fairly critical of McGovern. Nixon had someone in authority favorable to his cause at an influential newspaper, according to a conversation three weeks before the election. Haldeman told the president that a news executive knew of an FBI leak to a reporter at the newspaper. Haldeman identified the leaker as Mark Felt, the second in command at the FBI, but he would not tell Nixon who the informant was, who the reporter was, or which newspaper was involved.[17]

After the break-in, Nixon held five press conferences before the election. The first was on June 22 with only a few reporters in his office, not a full-blown conference. Nixon explained that reporters had complained that press conferences were dominated by foreign and defense policy discussions so he decided to have a smaller press conference with questions just on domestic affairs. In response to the only inquiry about Watergate, Nixon answered, "The White House has had no involvement whatever in this particular incident." Earlier, Ehrlichman had told reporters in Los Angeles that Nixon did not hold press conferences because reporters asked "dumb and flabby questions." At the June 22 gathering, Nixon generally disagreed with Ehrlichman's assessment, saying that smaller press conferences provide sharper questions and that was why he was holding a smaller one.[18] Later Nixon told Ehrlichman he was glad that Ehrlichman had accused reporters of asking such questions, because it put them on the defensive. Press conferences on June 29 and July 27 elicited not a single question about campaign finance irregularities or Watergate.

On August 29 at Nixon's home in San Clemente, California, the president held his fourth post-Watergate press conference and told reporters that there were minor technical campaign finance violations that were being corrected. He suggested that the Democrats had also committed violations under new laws. He said that there were many investigations of violations of campaign spending laws and the Watergate break-in. He said that Dean had conducted his own "thorough" investigation. "I can say categorically that his investigation indicates that no one in this Administration, presently employed, was involved in this very bizarre incident [Watergate] " He added later, "This kind of activity, as I have often indicated, has no place whatever in our political process. We want the air cleared. We want it cleared as soon as possible."[19] At an October 5 press conference, Nixon said charges that his administration was corrupt were political. He tried to tie Watergate accusations to complaints about his decisions that caused deaths in Vietnam. He said the FBI had carried out a thorough investigation and the rest should be left to a grand jury inquiry.[20] Reporters at five press conferences had posed three questions on Watergate in the four months following the burglary. The inquiries were scattered among a series of questions on other domestic and foreign policy matters and were quickly dismissed by the president.

As soon as the burglars were caught, Magruder, Liddy, and Strachan destroyed the White House files connected with the burglars. Hunt took ten thousand dollars from his White House safe. The five burglars plus Hunt and Liddy were indicted by a federal grand jury on September 15, 1972. This actually gave comfort to the White House because no one beyond the seven had been touched by the court system after three months of investigations.

Nixon, Dean, and Haldeman met in the Oval Office that day (Nixon claimed during the Watergate investigation that he had never met Dean until Feburary 1973). "How did it all end up?" Haldeman asked Dean. "Uh, I think, we can say 'well,' at this point. The, the press is playing it just as we expect," Dean answered. Haldeman said that the public would not think there was a whitewash because the seven had been indicted and "to those in the country, Liddy and Hunt are big men."[21]

NEWSPAPER AND MAGAZINE COVERAGE

Throughout the summer and autumn of 1972 Woodward and Bernstein pursued stories about Watergate, almost daily uncovering new angles about illicit funding, eavesdropping, and covert activities. In October, they discovered that many dirty tricks had been played on candidates who sought to oppose Nixon and they learned of Segretti's involvement. Other newspapers and news magazines picked up on the theme of the break-in being part of a panorama of dirty tricks and heavy cash payments to conspirators by using unidentified Justice Department sources. That seemed to be a turning point for the *Post*. It became clear that the break-in at the Democratic National Committee headquarters was not an isolated incident, and the newspapers' editors bore in, while other newspapers published stories mostly based upon official sources. Even after Woodward and Bernstein incorrectly wrote on October 25 that Sloan had testified to the grand jury that Haldeman was one of the persons who controlled the White House slush fund, the *Post* never wavered. It turned out that Haldeman did help control the funding, but Sloan had never testified to that effect because no one had asked him that question. The White House, meanwhile, remained publicly silent about the seven men indicted on conspiracy charges and stonewalled inquiries by federal authorities or reporters. The trial of the conspirators was scheduled to begin in January 1973.

In their book, Woodward and Bernstein alleged that no one else was pursuing the Watergate story. With four research assistants (see Acknowledgments), the author tested this argument.

Watergate articles and editorials in fifteen newspapers in major cities all over the United States published between June 18 and December 31, 1972, were tallied and categorized. Articles from the three national news magazines were also collected. The articles were categorized as to whether they were written by the newspaper's own reporters (staff news stories), by Associated Press or United Press International writers (wire stories), or by newspaper syndicate sources such as the *Los Angeles Times, New York Times,* or *Washington Post* wire service staffs. Finally the number of house editorials (editorials written as an expression of opinion of the newspaper) and the number of personal columns by local or syndicated columnists were categorized. Not included in the counts were letters to the editor or editorial cartoons because letters are random and not necessarily indicative of the newspaper's interest in the subject and because editorial cartoons usually accompanied editorials anyway and were sparse in number.

The newspapers were selected for geographic, political, and ideological balance. Consequently, this sampling was not just a list of the top fifteen newspapers by circulation, but a list of the largest newspapers as they represented their regions and various political leanings (see Appendix A for the listing of newspapers and the number of articles and editorials that appeared in each category for each newspaper).

Empirically, the numbers indicate that Woodward and Bernstein and the *Washington Post* accounted for a large portion of the printed Watergate information among the fifteen sampled newspapers in the second half of 1972. Staff news stories in that time frame published in the *Washington Post* and mostly written by Woodward and Bernstein totaled 201. Articles written by reporters from the fourteen other newspapers, including those written by the huge Washington Bureau staff of the *New York Times,* totaled 315, with 99 coming from just the *New York Times.* Among the fifteen sampled newspapers, the *Washington Post* accounted for 39 percent of the staff-generated stories in late 1972, the *New York Times* 19 percent, and the thirteen other newspapers 42 percent.

If the numbers of wire service and syndicated articles are added, 1,160 news articles appeared in the fifteen newspapers over those 6½ months. The *Washington Post* carried only four non–staff generated articles and the *New York Times* just seven. The share of Watergate news stories from those two leading newspapers drops to a combined 27 percent, 18 percent for the *Washington Post* and 9 percent for the *New York Times.* Of course, many of the syndicated stories in the other newspapers actually originated with the two leading newspapers and were picked up one cycle or one day later, so the influence of the *Washington Post* and the *New York Times* is understated by the 27 percent figure. The *Los Angeles Times,* for instance, carried thirty-two articles by Woodward and Bernstein during the summer and autumn of 1972, almost as many articles as was generated by its own staff (45). Editorials and columns point again to a much heavier *Washington Post* influence than that of any other newspaper. The *Post* published seventeen house editorials (26 percent of the 66 total) and fourteen columns of personal opinion (13 percent of the 108 total).

The *Los Angeles Times* carried more house editorials than the *New York Times* (13 to 10), and they both carried only two personal columns each on Watergate.

More telling than the empirical analysis, however, is the qualitative study of the fifteen newspapers' coverage of Watergate. Many of the *Washington Post* stories were carried on page one. After the initial few weeks following the break-in, Watergate stories appeared on page one in most of the other newspapers only occasionally. The *Washington Post* articles were often investigative in nature, even after the 1972 election, and revealed new details about covert activities directed by the White House. Other newspapers rarely carried their own enterprise stories. Often when they did carry such articles, the thrusts were superficial, misleading, or just plain wrong. Just after the Watergate burglary, the *New York Times*, for instance, tried to tie the burglars to the Bay of Pigs invasion in 1961, because of CIA connections and because most of the burglars were of Cuban extraction.

Political leanings appeared to play a role in the newspapers' decisions to publish information about Watergate. In the city of Chicago, the *Sun-Times* carried ninety articles, editorials, and columns on Watergate. The more conservative *Tribune* published sixty, or just two-thirds of the *Sun-Times* volume. Many of the *Sun-Times* articles were reprints of Woodward and Bernstein's stories picked up through the *Post* wire service. The *Wall Street Journal* published just eighteen articles and no columns or editorials, the *New Orleans Times-Picayune* published twenty-two articles and one personal column with no house editorials, and the *Houston Post* just forty-four articles, no editorials, and fourteen columns of personal opinion. Most of the Houston newspaper's articles were far inside the newspaper, and many were generated through the *Chicago Tribune* wire service. The few staff-generated articles dealt with threats by the chair of the House Banking Committee to launch a Watergate investigation. The chair, Democratic Representative Wright Patman, was from Texas, and so the *Houston Post* was close to him. Unfortunately for Patman and the newspaper, members of his committee, including six Democrats, refused to support the investigation and voted it down in early October.

Coverage in the more liberal newspapers was extensive. The *Los Angeles Times* carried 136 articles and opinion pieces, the *Detroit Free Press* 110, and the *San Francisco Chronicle* 110, although there were no *Chronicle* editorials and only three columns. The *Chronicle* and the *Los Angeles Times* picked up most of their Watergate material from the *Washington Post* wire service or the national wire services.

The national newsmagazines followed the same trend. *U.S. News & World Report* published only one article on Watergate in the summer and autumn of 1972. Appearing in the September 25 edition, the article, "What the 'Watergate Case' Is All About,"[22] simply summarized without comment the public facts about Watergate that were generally known. *Time* carried nine articles and *Newsweek* eight. These articles focused on the unfolding facts about the backgrounds of the burglars and occasionally delved into specifics about various investigations, including what FBI agents were learning in their investigations for the Justice Department.

Most of the stories from the newspapers other than the *Washington Post* resulted from interviews with Washington officials, from press conferences, or from court actions. That is, they stayed with easily accessible but partisan sources such as Ziegler, Democratic Party Chair Lawrence O'Brien, or some local congressman well known to the newspaper.

This kind of coverage and the indictment of only the five burglars and Hunt and Liddy on September 15 put the Nixon inner circle at ease. Most of the country had not heard of Watergate. On October 19, Godfrey Sperling Jr., a reporter for the *Christian Science Monitor*, published the results of his two-day polling of newspaper editors all over the country. Sperling wrote: "But, by and large, and including the Northeast, *Monitor* political observers polled on this question found no evidence that the issue had emerged as a major one in the presidential campaign.... Almost all the *Monitor* observers said they, themselves, were surprised that the charges had not become an issue." He also wrote that his observers were telling him that generally people thought this kind of underhanded activity occurred all the time, that Nixon supporters just did not believe that Nixon had anything to do with the covert activities, and that Watergate was just too complicated to excite voters.[23]

Meanwhile, the White House's counteroffensive against the *Washington Post* heated up in October. There was a lull in Watergate coverage in other newspapers and the national newsmagazines just before the election, but the *Post* continued its daily coverage. On October 18, a day before the *Monitor's* survey was released, the *Post's* editorial writers were moved to defend the newspaper's coverage. "The charges really hinge on the question of whether there is something going on here that the people should know about," the editorial writer opined. The editorial then pointed out that Woodward and Bernstein had "carefully checked each story and that the information was not irresponsible, could be confirmed by supplementary information, and was from sources who were in a position to know what they were talking about." The editorial denounced White House attacks on the press and called for more candor from all sides.[24]

There were a few exceptions to the official sourcing. On October 4, the *New York Times* reported that Dwight Chapin, Nixon's appointments secretary, had been linked to Segretti and the dirty tricks campaign (Segretti had indeed been recruited by Chapin). On December 10, E. Howard Hunt's wife, Dorothy, was killed in a plane crash in Chicago. In her purse, investigators found more than $10,000 in cash. News media quickly picked up on this story, creating an ominous end-of-the-year atmosphere for the White House. On December 19, John F. Lawrence, the *Los Angeles Times* bureau chief, was jailed for refusing to give U.S. District Judge John Sirica the tapes of an interview with Watergate figure Alfred C. Baldwin III (Baldwin had been a lookout for the burglars). Lawrence was jailed for two days until Baldwin's attorneys allowed him to release the tapes to Sirica. Two other reporters, Jack Nelson and Ronald J. Ostrow, had interviewed Baldwin and written stories earlier in the month, but Lawrence was in charge of the tapes. This, too, gathered media interest.

Television coverage was sparse, with occasional stories about Watergate figures and public statements, but by and large the Watergate puzzle was too complex for dissection in the broadcast media. There were too few reporters and too little airtime for such an investigation and for so difficult a story to unearth against the wishes of the Nixon administration.

It is not true that no one besides the *Washington Post* pursued the Watergate story. More than 1,100 articles and opinion pieces appeared in surveyed major newspapers and newsmagazines nationwide—not a large number but more than probably most would have guessed. Editorials called for more candor and a clearing of the air. One of the strongest reasons for the lack of interest in Watergate was a common assumption that it was a minor caper contained to the lowest levels of the administration, which, of course, was what Nixon, Haldeman, and Ehrlichman wanted the public to believe. No one, not even the *Post* staffers, were quite certain where exactly this story would lead, who was involved, and what the implications were. It is true that Woodward and Bernstein seemed to be the only two reporters who pursued every aspect of the break-in, the dirty tricks, and money-laundering campaigns, and the illegal wiretapping, but even they had no idea until late in 1972 what they were on to.

What other reasons prompted the media, except for the *Washington Post*, to pursue the Watergate story indifferently in late 1972? One obvious one was that the election campaign was in full swing and McGovern was trying to capitalize on the story. No news organization wanted to appear to be too enthusiastic about Watergate, not knowing what the result of the investigation might be. The ever-watchful White House had somewhat cowed opinion makers and reporters, but there was also the tradition of trying to stay neutral in coverage of a presidential election. Without a smoking gun, the media was queasy about pursuing a scandal involving a presidential candidate, especially one who was about to be reelected by a landslide.

But there was also the style of reporting that had overtaken Washington. After World War II, political bias was not so apparent in news coverage as it had been when individual newspaper magnates controlled the industry. Still, reporters had come to rely on press conferences and official sources or on mixing with legislators and White House staffers at dinners and cocktail parties, where story leads and gossip could provide enterprise stories. The White House had slapped a lid on such conversations in 1972, and Woodward and Bernstein were too young and too idealistic to know or even care that this was how the game was played. They simply pressed secretaries, assistants, clerical staffers, and other lower-echelon personnel to put bits and pieces together. They kept stringing together random bits of information until a murky picture began to appear.

Left at the gate, other reporters could not catch up to Woodward and Bernstein. Without a phalanx of sources and information, it was impossible to intrude on Woodward's and Bernstein's investigation. At the same time, by coincidence (or maybe not by coincidence), Woodward and Bernstein rarely had any sources on the record in their stories, allowing no other medium to contact those sources and use the *Post* stories as leads for their own sourcing and investigations.

The two reporters claimed that all their stories were confirmed by at least two separate sources and that all stories were checked and rechecked. Indeed, little that they wrote was ever challenged, but that kind of investigative reporting was new. Most investigative stories are based upon documents that other reporters have either missed or could not find. Basing damaging and potentially libelous stories upon what sources said is an unusual and dangerous game. This kind of reporting, even in the most respected newspapers would become common, but the care that Woodward and Bernstein showed would not be there. In a roundabout way, the two reporters began a genre of reporting suited to their abilities, but not fitted to most correspondents' talents. In fact, later investigations by Woodward began to tatter his reputation because the unidentified sources were not always as reliable as in 1972.

Also, the other media did not pursue the story because Washington is the most competitive news town in the country and perhaps the world. No respectable reporter wanted to trail along eating dust and picking up droppings, trying to compete with two in-town reporters who clearly had the inside track. Better to just leave the story alone and let the two *Post* reporters sink or swim.

Finally, there is the psychology of the times. As has been pointed out, Americans generally wanted Nixon to succeed as president. They were tired of the turmoil of the 1960s and wanted a calmer situation. Nixon was about to end American participation in the war in Southeast Asia and campus disturbances had quieted since the spring of 1970. World War II–generation voters believed or had been led to believe that the real enemies were longhaired protesters and the liberal news media. Watergate was a fiction created by the malevolent media, the worst of which was the *Washington Post*. In this way, the public still bought into the White House logic: Nixon was a victim, not a predator. When the truth came out and the roles were reversed, the effect upon an already disillusioned public (by Vietnam) was incalculable.

This 6½-month period in late 1972 has been romanticized because of a best-selling book and a motion picture, *All the President's Men*. In truth, it is, in many ways, the least important time period of the Nixon presidency. A major scandal was largely ignored and an election was held under false pretenses. Woodward and Bernstein kept the story alive—that is the significance of this time period and that is what ensured their places in history.

But the real impact of Watergate would not be felt until 1973 and 1974 when the court system and Congress became actively involved. All of this would be brought into living rooms, where it could not be ignored. But it would be television and not the *Washington Post* that would help spell Nixon's end.

NOTES

1. Richard Nixon, *The Memoirs of Richard Nixon* (New York: Grosset & Dunlap, 1978), 335.

2. John Ehrlichman, *Witness to Power* (New York: Simon & Schuster, 1982), 342–43.

3. Nixon, Dean, and Haldeman conversation in the Oval Office, *U.S. vs. John Mitchell et al.*, exhibit 12 (original Watergate tape), 16.

4. H.R. Haldeman, *The Ends of Power* (New York: New York Times Books, 1978), 155–72.

5. H.R. Haldeman, *The Haldeman Diaries: Inside the Nixon White House* (New York: G.P. Putnam's Sons, 1994), boxed addendum after June 18, 1972, entry, 472.

6. Charles Colson, *Born Again* (Old Tappan, N.J.: Chosen Books, 1972), 68–72.

7. FBI Special Agent Angelo J. Lano, report of interview with Jeb Stuart Magruder, March 14, 1973, p. 3, University of Illinois Library, Nixon-Watergate microfilm collection, Urbana, Illinois.

8. Nixon and Haldeman, Executive Office Building conversation, June 20, 1972, Abuse of Government Power tapes (released in 1996).

9. Nixon and Haldeman, Oval Office conversation, June 23, 1972, *U.S. vs. Mitchell et al.*, Exhibit 35 (one of the "smoking gun" tapes originally released).

10. Nixon and Haldeman, Executive Office Building conversation, June 26, 1972, Nixon Tapes.

11. Nixon and Haldeman, Oval Office conversation, June 30, 1972, Nixon Tapes.

12. Nixon and Ehrlichman, Oval Office conversation, July 19, 1972.

13. Nixon, *The Memoirs of Richard Nixon*, 646.

14. Nixon, dictation at Camp David, August 9, 1972, Nixon Tapes.

15. Nixon and Haldeman, Oval Office conversation, September 8, 1972, Nixon Tapes.

16. Nixon and Haldeman, Oval Office conversation of October 15, 1972.

17. Nixon and Haldeman, Executive Office Building conversation, October 19, 1972, Nixon Tapes.

18. George W. Johnson, *The Nixon Presidential Press Conferences* (New York: Earl M. Coleman, 1978), June 22 Press Conference, 248, 250–51.

19. Johnson, *Nixon Presidential Press Conferences*, "The President's News Conference of August 29, 1972, 280–82. Also see "Press Conference No. 27 of the President of the United States," Ziegler Papers, Box 16, Watergate file, 1–2.

20. Johnson, *Nixon Presidential Press Conferences*, "The President's News Conference of October 5, 1972, 291, 295–296.

21. Nixon Haldeman, and Dean, Oval Office conversation, September 15, 1972, *U.S. vs. Mitchell et al.* tape.

22. "What the 'Watergate Case' Is All About," *U.S. News & World Report*, September 25, 1972, 27–29.

23. Godfrey Sperling Jr., *Christian Science Monitor*, "Ethics charges largely ignored," October 19, 1972, 1, 6.

24. "Alarms, Diversions—and Responsibilities," *Washington Post* editorial, October 18, 1972, A16.

Chapter 6

The Tapes

As his second term began, the public's perception of Richard Nixon differed significantly from how he would be seen only a year later. In January 1973 voters saw him as a highly successful politician who had been reelected easily, only the third president since World War I to win a second term on his own. They saw a man who had beaten his critics and who had fought a Democrat-controlled House and Senate to a standstill. By the end of 1973, they would see a beaten man who was marking time until his resignation.

Nixon, Chief of Staff H. R. Haldeman, and domestic advisor John Ehrlichman felt comfortable, if not confident, in January 1973, so the White House inner circle spent its time planning harassing strategies against perceived enemies. They discussed denying *Washington Post* reporters access to the White House, challenging the FCC licenses of two television stations owned by the *Post* company, and launching a public relations offensive to obliterate any negative, lingering Watergate images. They also reflected on their mistakes. Nixon told aide Charles Colson on January 2 that involving White House staff directly in the dirty tricks campaign led by Donald Segretti had been a bad idea. Colson responded simply: "The mistake of the Watergate was whoever said, 'Do it.'"[1]

At the same time, everyone in the Oval Office feared what might happen. Only seven persons had been implicated in the Watergate break-in—the five burglars plus the masterminds, G. Gordon Liddy and E. Howard Hunt—but the White House knew that if any of the seven talked, the entire administration would be endangered. At first, there seemed to be nothing to worry about. As the burglars' pretrial appearances began, they remained silent. The money found in Dorothy Hunt's purse after the Chicago crash had not been traced definitively to anyone beyond the seven defendants either. Although Hunt was blackmailing the White House (the money in the purse had led to other demands), the strategy of enforced silence appeared to be a success. Two weeks before the inauguration, Haldeman told Nixon and Ehrlichman that Hunt would take a guilty plea. "They will ask him presumably, whether there were any higher-ups involved after he takes his guilty plea, and he'll say no, and he'll go to jail," the chief of staff said. Haldeman added that Liddy would plead not guilty, though he knew that probably he would be convicted. Liddy was hoping to find a trial error that would get him off on a technicality. James McCord was expected to testify, but he would not involve anyone else and all seven defendants would refuse to testify before Congress after their trials, if they were subpoenaed, Haldeman said.[2]

True to his word, on January 11 Hunt pled guilty, telling the court that no one in the White House was involved in the break-in. On January 15, four of the five burglars—Bernard L. Barker, Eugenio R. Martinez, Frank Sturgis, and Virgilio R. Gonzales—also pled guilty and on January 30 both McCord, the fifth burglar, and Liddy were found guilty. Liddy did not get his trial error and none of the defendants indicated that anyone beyond the accused was involved. Judge John Sirica set sentencing for March.

Meanwhile, Congress had activated its own Watergate investigation. On February 7, the Senate voted to authorize the creation of a select committee to investigate possible malfeasance in the Nixon administration. The committee, which came to be known as the Watergate Committee or the Ervin Committee, began issuing subpoenas in March under the direction of Chair Sam Ervin, a Democrat from North Carolina. In May, Attorney General Elliot Richardson appointed Archibald Cox, a Harvard law professor, special counsel to unearth and prosecute malfeasance related to the burglary. Significantly, Cox was a special counsel, not an independent counsel, which meant that he answered to Richardson, who technically answered to Nixon, setting up a potential conflict of interest. Now there were three sets of sleuths hounding Nixon: Woodward and Bernstein, Sirica, and the Watergate Committee.

Still, if the seven did not crack, the investigations would come to nothing. The White House left nothing to chance. The president chose John Dean to plan White House strategy. Dean had been legal counsel to the president for three years and was regarded as a rising star in the Nixon coterie. So that there would be no mistake about who would plan strategy, Haldeman wrote to Colson: "John Dean is handling the entire Watergate matter now and any questions or input you have should be directed to him and no one else."[3] Colson had a way of freelancing when inquiries came around or if action were needed. Haldeman knew it was long past the time when the White House could tolerate characters ad-libbing their lines.

There were other practical reasons for the Dean appointment. It was time, Haldeman reasoned, for others in the White House to start planning legislative and administrative strategies for the second term. Haldeman noted in his diary that the White House's key challenge in February 1973 was to get everybody (White House, Congress, and press) to get along and to avoid confrontations. "It isn't us that's confronting," he added in his notes indicating that the press was at fault. "Mistake for P [Nixon] to take on press—unites them. Instead should do things to get msg [message] thru," he wrote.[4]

Though disaster was looming, Haldeman's notes clearly indicate that ten weeks before he was forced to resign, Watergate was not high on his list of things to worry about and that Dean, not he or Nixon, would have to spend the sleepless nights conjuring steps to be taken in the cover-up. He wrote years later: "The Watergate break-in, and the associated revelations of Woodward and Bernstein, had failed to ignite the public. And now Nixon, a President more feared by Democrats and the bureaucracy than any President in this century was at the peak of his power with control of the government tightly in his hands."[5] A Vietnam truce had been signed in January, heralding the post-Vietnam era in America. The Nixon White House now had the chance to address an agenda that did not include a debilitating conflict halfway around the world, and no one in the Nixon inner circle wanted that time in history spoiled by a minor prank at the Watergate office complex. Even years after the dust had settled, Haldeman did not understand how much had occurred that made Nixon's resignation likely.

In early 1973, though, Haldeman was shortsighted or just purposefully optimistic. Watergate would not go away, and it was naïve for him to think that the burglars would quietly accept prison sentences without implicating anyone else. What he should have realized, and the rest of the White House should have known, was that unreliable characters such as Hunt, Liddy, and McCord held the future of the Nixon administration in their hands. And that was why the path of the scandal was inevitable. Colson was only partially correct in his January remarks to Nixon. The real mistake was whoever said: "Pay Liddy and Hunt to make sure we win." Playing hardball was one thing, but giving a free hand for wild acts of subterfuge to such unprincipled amateurs was just plain stupid. And now in the spring of 1973 everyone concerned would begin to pay the price.

Matters deteriorated quickly in March and April. On March 10, Colson, having just returned from a trip to Eastern Europe on Nixon's behalf, was forced to resign because it was feared that investigators knew too much about Colson's role in the Ellsberg break-in. Haldeman ordered Dean to keep Colson on the payroll as a consultant so that executive privilege would still cover Colson, supposedly protecting him from subpoenas to testify.[6] Colson eventually pleaded guilty to obstruction of justice in June 1974 in connection with the break-in at Lewis Fielding's Beverly Hills office (Daniel Ellsberg's psychiatrist) and was sentenced to one to three years in prison and fined $5,000. He served seven months before being paroled.

In April 1973, the Senate refused to confirm L. Patrick Gray as permanent FBI director because Nixon would not allow Dean to testify about Gray's possible role in the Watergate cover-up. Nixon issued a statement on April 5 after the Senate refused to confirm Gray: "Because I asked my counsel, John Dean, to conduct a thorough investigation of alleged involvement in the Watergate episode, Director Gray was asked to make FBI reports available to Mr. Dean. His compliance with this completely proper and necessary request exposed Mr. Gray to totally unfair innuendo and suspicion, and thereby seriously tarnished his fine record. ... I have regretfully agreed to withdraw Mr. Gray's nomination."[7] Nixon did not explain why he would not let Dean testify about Gray. Gray resigned as acting director on April 27 after it was revealed that he had destroyed documents.

The White House strategy to leave everything to Dean changed quickly. Nixon felt it was time to plan strategy, so he met with Dean on March 21 and, in a wide-ranging conversation that lasted over two hours and that takes up more than one hundred pages of manuscript, Dean laid out the president's options. He explained the extent of the cover-up and the details of who did what. He also suggested that Nixon attempt to eradicate the "cancer on the presidency" before it spread. Dean's warnings were prophetic. They also provided a basis by which prosecutors could prove that Nixon knew in detail about the cover-up. Nixon later described the conversation as the first time he heard some of the details of Watergate, and he argued that it was a catalyst for his personal intervention to rectify the wrongs that had been committed. That was a prevarication, disproved over and over again by the tapes and by testimony from other Watergate figures. Nixon planned the cover-up from the time that he returned from Key Biscayne in June 1972 and probably authorized the June 17 burglary. The March 21, 1973, conversation, while damning in itself, was only one of a series of implicating conversations in the year after the burglary. The White House's worst fears were soon to be realized.

Two days later, McCord, facing a long prison term, sent a note to Sirica telling him that he had been ordered to remain silent and that perjury had been committed. The inevitable hole in the dike appeared. Sirica read the note in court, and the media began following Watergate events more closely. McCord testified again before the grand jury. Sirica handed the defendants long prison terms and ordered that the grand jury investigation be expanded. Nixon's inner circle stopped talking about courses of action to be taken against enemies and concentrated on how to save themselves by blunting the Senate and federal court inquiries. Haldeman reflected in his diary that he now saw signs of the "domino theory," meaning that everyone might fall. He and Nixon worried about whether they could really trust Dean to handle the investigations and whether Dean himself would keep quiet.

To make matters worse, Vice President Spiro Agnew faced increasingly serious problems of his own. While governor of Maryland in 1966, Agnew had been involved in financial irregularities surrounding the construction of a horse racetrack. Agnew called Haldeman on April 10 to warn him of possible trouble. On October 10 Agnew pleaded nolo contendere in federal court to one count of failing to report income to the Internal Revenue Service, ostensibly from illicit income not reported on tax returns. He then resigned as vice president.

Meanwhile, Dean sensed the White House's softened support for his Watergate strategy. Fearing he would be sacrificed as a scapegoat, he spoke to prosecutors about a deal, engendering the wrath of Nixon, Haldeman, and Ehrlichman, according to taped White House conversations. But the anger led nowhere. Events were spinning out of control. On April 23, Ziegler told Ehrlichman and Haldeman that, though Nixon believed in their innocence, they both needed to leave the White House so that Nixon could move in a new direction.[8] Nixon spoke to them personally on April 30, affirming that they would have to quit. The investigation had pointed toward the president's two key advisors and, without hesitation, Nixon cut them loose. Attorney General Richard Kleindeinst and Dean also resigned that day. With less than four months expired in the second term, Nixon's entire inner circle was gone and it was clear that Dean would tell all he knew.

The president spoke on national television that night. Nixon took the occasion to watch out for his own interests. He said that he had been assured many times by his staff that no one in the White House had authorized the Watergate burglary. He said that new information had come to him, ostensibly from Dean on March 21, and that he personally had taken over investigation of the matter. He revealed that the four administration leaders had resigned that day. "In any organization, the man at the top must bear the responsibility. That responsibility, therefore, belongs here, in this office. I accept it. And I pledge to you tonight, from this office, that I will do everything in my power to ensure that the guilty are brought to justice, and that such abuses are purged from our political processes in the years to come, long after I have left this office."[9]

Nixon, of course, had once again lied. He certainly knew all the Watergate details after his June 23, 1972, conversation and probably had authorized the second break-in on June 17. His claim to have first learned about Watergate on March 21, 1973, was an effort to throw the blame onto others. As has been pointed out, the value of the tapes released in 1996 is that they clearly show that Nixon had many conversations over the months after the burglary in which he discussed and sometimes planned cover-up strategy. Contrary to his claim in his speech, he was trying to place responsibility on anyone and everyone else. It was always someone else. The Kennedys and their money. The press and their snobby, high-handed malignant reporting. The Democrats and their sniveling liberal attitudes. A group of enemies who appreciated neither Nixon's talents nor the people he represented. Always in his long career in Washington, others made the mistakes, in Nixon's estimation. Someone else's fault. Nixon really believed that he was an innocent victim of his enemies. His impassioned statements that he would stay in office and never walk away were not just calculated bursts of bombast, but eruptions of malignancy from his inner soul and true representations of his determination to fight on in the face of overwhelming odds against him. If he had ever slightly stepped over the line, it was only to fight fire with fire, Nixon rationalized. He would win, because the American public would see past the "minor" escapades to a man who was trying to do good.

But the significance of that day's events rested with the resignations. They marked the infiltration of Watergate damage to the highest levels of the administration, just short of the president himself. This was only weeks after Haldeman had been trying to organize White House affairs and ignore Watergate. April 30's announcements also meant that Nixon virtually had to start over, assembling a new staff of people he neither knew well nor was comfortable with. Henry Kissinger became secretary of state in September, replacing William Rogers, while Alexander Haig immediately assumed the duties of chief of staff and Ronald Ziegler took charge of the entire White House information system, in fact if not in name. This brought the press secretary into Nixon's inner circle for the first time, but it did not improve press relations.

The stress was felt widely by reporters. One of them, Jerry Landay, had joined the Washington bureau of the American Broadcasting Company in 1972. A veteran newsman, Landay did hourly radio broadcasts nationwide and filled in on the television side occasionally. "You could sense a certain understanding [among the press corps] that tension was building," Landay said of the spring of 1973. "There was a certain degree of correctness always in the air, but never was Ziegler forthcoming."

Landay had smelled what was coming the day the burglars were arrested. "I led all morning with the arrests," he said. "My boss [Kenneth Scott, director of ABC radio operations in Washington] called me from home and asked me why I was leading with the break-in story. I told him, 'I have a journalist's hunch in the seat of my pants and I think this story is important.'" Landay said a burglary at the Democratic National Headquarters had to be politically connected because the burglars could not have been seeking money or valuables in the office. "From the time the connection was made between the burglars and the White House, there was a sense of inevitability," Landay said.[10] So the questions from the reporters to Ziegler got tougher and tougher, and his elevation in the White House apparatus only furthered reporters' distrust of the young press secretary.

Ziegler, previously shunned by the official inner circle, increasingly became the target of White House correspondents' wrath. Haig had been vice chief of staff of the Army and Kissinger a useful but often ridiculed and spied-upon foreign affairs advisor. As the last months of his presidency began, Nixon could place his confidence in no one and he could not get advice he valued, because his chief advisors now were people he would neither have faith in nor confide in.

WATERGATE HEARINGS

The public resignations of Nixon's most trusted advisors stirred the country. Until May 1973 the country had viewed Watergate as a political matter involving jealous party officials on both sides, a minor scandal of interest only to those working inside the Beltway, the freeway circling Washington. Suddenly, even Nixon conceded that there was more to it. The public took more curious note of what was occurring on Pennsylvania Avenue. Reporters who had ignored the unfolding scandal suddenly began devoting their energy to learning every detail.

And as the president fought on for another fifteen months, the country's business came to a virtual halt. Watergate occurred at an inopportune moment. The long, post–World War II era of U.S. prosperity was ending. Inflation started to erode corporate profits and personal prosperity. The stock market dropped 40 percent in value between 1972 and 1974. By the end of the decade, thousands of businesses had closed, unemployment had risen to uncomfortable levels, and spiraling inflation had taken a heavy toll on personal income. In June 1973, Nixon ordered a freeze on all wages and prices nationwide to dampen inflation, an artificial cap that was usually used during wartime. The experiment lasted only a short time and, when the lid was lifted, prices spiraled upward. The middle-class American dream of a home, two cars, college educations for the children, summer vacations, and guaranteed employment was ending. The war in Vietnam and social welfare programs enacted in the 1960s had drained the treasury. The president and Congress needed to work in concert to preserve the economy and prop up America's place in the world, but instead Washington immersed itself in the Watergate mess. The inevitable toll on the public would be extracted over the next nine years.

But in the late spring of 1973, the president had no time for the economy. He was forced to defend himself against Watergate accusations. He told a group of Republicans at a fund-raising dinner on May 9: "I can assure you that we will get to the bottom of this very deplorable incident [Watergate]. ... But the most important thing I want to say tonight is this: We are not going to allow this deplorable incident to deter us or deflect us from going forward toward achieving the great goals that an overwhelming majority of the American people elected us to achieve in November of 1972." Nixon again spoke to the public on May 22, saying that the CIA had been involved in the Watergate investigation, but that the involvement was not political. Haldeman pointed to this speech later as a major blunder on Nixon's part because Nixon should have realized that the tapes would become public eventually and reveal just the opposite. The web of lies started to strangle the imprisoned president.[11]

What prompted the May 22 speech was Nixon's slow recognition that he would have to explain the covert activities that led up to the burglary at the Watergate complex. He had never dreamed he would have to deal with his dirty laundry publicly, especially his having used the CIA to block an FBI investigation. By claiming May 22 that the March 21 conversation with Dean had changed his outlook on Watergate (though he continued to allege he was innocent of any wrongdoing), Nixon allowed a small part of the truth to become public. That fact is what made the revelation of the existence of the tapes crucial, because prosecutors sensed that the rest of the story lay buried somewhere and the tapes would be the vehicles by which they would learn the real truth.

Only Nixon, Haldeman, Haldeman aide Alexander Butterfield, and four Secret Service agents knew about the existence of the tapes. What would happen
if the existence of the tapes became more widely known? Nixon wondered. He
worried that too much had been recorded. On April 9, he and Haldeman decided
to discontinue the voice activation of the tapes at their various locations. From
that day forward, Nixon could turn on the tapes, but he would be more careful
about taping conversations, especially telephone conversations. He stopped the
recordings altogether in July 1973. If the tapes reached open court, Nixon's
carefully nurtured image as a president who was a victim of a liberal establishment and a hostile press might come crashing to earth. Still, he was confident
enough that executive privilege would protect him from the release of the tapes
that, by and large, Nixon left the tapes in tact. He also claimed later that his decision not to destroy the tapes was based upon legal advice.

Three days after his decision to cut back on the use of the tapes, he talked
about his misgivings and his continuing faith that certain media organizations
might do his bidding in restoring Haldeman's image. "It seems to me we ought
to try and get the [Chicago] *Trib* and anybody else that will run a story [to
write] about the real Bob Haldeman and the kids," Nixon told Ehrlichman, perhaps out of guilt as much as sorrow.[12] Though Haldeman had resigned, Nixon
talked frankly with him by telephone throughout May about the cover-up and
how to continue to keep a lid on the details. At the same time, the president insisted to Haig that he knew nothing of covert activities the tapes reveal. Nixon
could not speak honestly with his new advisors, but he kept up a frank dialogue
with his departed ones.

Nixon's relationship with Haldeman had been businesslike. Nixon hardly
knew how to relate to those around him on a personal level. He was a solitary
individual, who took vacations with political associates and friends, while leaving his family at home. His life was his political career. But as the time came for
him to ask for his chief of staff's resignation, Nixon showed rare personal an-
guish. He felt remorse about Haldeman's forced resignation and for what
surely was in store for his most trusted aide.

But even the most sympathetic newspapers and magazines had begun to
question Nixon's role by this time, and Nixon's reasoning that he could plant
favorable stories on Haldeman's behalf revealed a lack of understanding of
what was occurring. Five days later on May 5, though, the insight grew. Ziegler
told reporters that day that previous Watergate statements from the press office were "inoperative," which was Zieglerese to explain that some of the White
House's previous explanations had been lies. "Well, it will be a great day on the
other side for all of our enemies, won't it? The *Times*, the *Post*, the rest—shit,"
Nixon told Kissinger late that night.

Still, Nixon found it hard to believe that a public who had handed him a re-
sounding election victory just a half year earlier could have changed their
minds so quickly. Nixon clung to the notion that journalistic observers and voters alike really wanted him to remain president and that only a small adjust-

ment in press strategy would bring most journalists to his defense. He sought consolation from Ziegler. "But, tell me this, in spite of all their vindictiveness and so forth, they—the press—still wants [*sic*] the President to come out all right?" Nixon asked. Ziegler avoided answering the question.[13] Nixon came to realize in the coming weeks why Ziegler would not answer.

On May 20, Nixon remarked that, for eight weeks, the Sunday newspapers had been carrying long Watergate summaries and ignoring other news. He told Ziegler that attacks on Haldeman and Ehrlichman were really attempts to get him. That was the entire focus of both Congress and the media, Nixon said, taking the opposite point of view from his conversation on April 27. Ziegler disagreed, speaking out this time. "My view is that is not a correct assumption to assume that all of the Congress and all of the press have the objective of destroying the President," Ziegler answered. Nixon backed down somewhat: "I didn't mean all. No."[14]

Nixon escaped the Watergate mess briefly in June by holding the Strategic Arms Limitation Talks with Soviet Premier Leonid Brezhnev at Camp David, Maryland. Nixon was eager to build on the historic SALT treaty reached in 1972 (the treaty has remained in effect for more than 30 years). The summit meeting ended in concurrence on such issues as agricultural exports, transportation, oceanic studies, taxation, commercial aviation, the peaceful use of atomic energy, and trade, but not in the sweeping nuclear arms compromises that the president hoped would draw attention away from Watergate. Nixon wrote later that more progress could not be made because of conservative opposition in Congress and "Zionist" opposition in the face of restrictive Soviet emigration policies for Jews seeking to leave the Soviet Union.[15] But perhaps Nixon's weakened position had played a part in the Soviet strategy. The meeting with Brezhnev allowed the president to use his diplomatic skills and unparalleled acumen for finding common ground with which to forge future international agreements, but Nixon could not take much comfort in those theoretical triumphs.

After Brezhnev left, the president was forced to deal once again with Watergate. The Senate Committee hearings had opened already and the country tuned in to see if there was any substance to the allegations. Most of the hearings were seen on the national networks during the day, preempting soap operas, to the chagrin of some viewers. The seven-member committee paraded thirty-three Watergate figures into the Senate hearing room during thirty-seven days of testimony between May 17 and August 7, filling 237 hours of television coverage. The hearings continued into the fall, but the damage had been done by the first week in August. The witnesses included former White House staffers and members of CREEP such as James McCord, Howard Hunt, Gordan Liddy, Tony Ulasewicz, Jack Caulfield, John Ehrlichman, H. R. Haldeman, Job Magruder, and Maurice Stans. The highlight came at the end of June, when Dean testified, and again on July 16, when Alexander Butterfield appeared.

During the entire series of hearings the nation dropped most of its interest in local matters and turned to Washington. Historians Gladys Lang and Kurt Lang have written that the Watergate investigation was actually a battle for public opinion. Nixon could hang on to the office as long as he had public opinion behind him. Lang and Lang offer a rather interesting and complex series of arguments about how public opinion interacted with the unfolding Watergate scandal. The average U.S. home tuned into thirty hours of the hearings, with almost three-quarters of Americans watching some part of the hearings by the second week of testimony, according to Lang and Lang.[16] The two authors are correct, of course. The entire Watergate cover-up and investigation were all about public perceptions. As was discussed earlier, Nixon had portrayed himself as a victim of a vindictive and unyielding liberal establishment that included war protesters, liberals, and the media. Americans, by and large, had accepted that thesis.

That was why public opinion was so important. Attitudes had been tied to the White House's martyr strategy over the previous fifty-two months. If evidence suggested that Nixon and his administration were other than what had been depicted in their White House publicity campaigns, that they had been perpetrating a foul hoax on the public, the effect would be catastrophic for both Nixon and the presidency.

The Watergate era was not a time for disappointing the public. There had been too much disillusionment during the Vietnam conflict. For the nation's political institutions—particularly the presidency—to retain the confidence of the electorate, there had to be a heavy dose of honesty and reassurance, and public opinion had to remain on the side of the president—and the presidency. This did not happen. Watergate obliterated public trust in both the government and the presidency. Watergate piled upon Vietnam piled upon the 1970s revelations about John F. Kennedy's personal life heaped upon the public evidence about FBI wrongdoing in the 1960s created an unparalleled disillusionment with every facet of the national government, but particularly with the presidency.

TELEVISION'S WATERGATE ROLE

The process of disillusionment began in earnest in the summer of 1973, and television played a large part in the drama. Newspapers carried front-page headlines about Watergate for two months and newsmagazines followed the Senate testimony with the same intensity, but it was the revelations seen on living-room televisions across the country that spelled the end of the Nixon presidency and trouble for administrations of the future. If Watergate was a battle for public opinion, television was the battleground, and there was no way this time for Nixon to manipulate the coverage.

Woodward and Bernstein and the *Washington Post* had done their part in keeping the Watergate story alive, but in the summer of 1973 it was the televised hearings that perpetuated the drama. The *Post* continued to follow the story, of course, as did every newspaper in the country, but Woodward and Bernstein were no longer breaking the important new facts. Coverage was now controlled by official, public activities with all media closely reporting the story. This was not Watergate's most cinematic time (the June 17 to December period in 1972 resulted in the book and the movie *All the President's Men*), but it was certainly the most critical one.

An overwrought president did not react well to the pyramiding adversity. Nixon imagined press leaks everywhere. He told Ziegler of a letter from Ehrlichman that accused Nixon's attorney, Leonard Garment, of leaking information to Bob Woodward and to Seymour Hersh of the *New York Times*. Nixon believed Ehrlichman, but Ziegler assured the president that Ehrlichman was wrong.[17] This did not placate the president in the least. The same day, Nixon told Colson by telephone that "this business of attacking the president has got to stop. . . . And as far as this press corps, they can go to hell." Still the toady, although he had been fired, Colson replied, "Oh sure. The hell with them, man. Mr. President, the great silent majority see right through them. My God, if you could, if you could see the mail that I've gotten this last week." Nixon answered: "Yeah, we've been on the defensive for two months, because, basically, you see, they were right, in a sense. There was a cover-up. Let's face it. Uhh, but on the other hand, they have built up first the crime and the cover-up to unbelievable things and of course the fact that people had to leave, a number of them."[18]

James McCord testified to the Watergate Committee on May 18 that he had been ordered to keep silent, basically offering the same testimony that he had given in his letter to Judge Sirica in March. White House operatives Jack Caulfield and Tony Ulasewicz told the committee they had obstructed justice. Jeb Stuart Magruder, CREEP deputy director, implicated Mitchell and Dean, among others, in the cover-up of the break-in. Prosecutor Archibald Cox announced on June 18 that he was investigating whether a sitting president could be subpoenaed or indicted.

Nixon fought back ineffectively. In anticipation of Dean's testimony, the White House leaked information that Dean had taken White House funds for use on his honeymoon. Nixon's strategy had shifted as he tried to blame the entire Watergate scandal on his former legal advisor, but the accusations against Dean and the meager White House efforts to discredit him paled in comparison to Dean's testimony.

Dean arrived on June 25 before the Senate Watergate Committee and testified for five days; the first day was taken up by his reading a prepared statement for seven hours. He told the committee about the March 21, 1973, conversation in which he warned Nixon about a cancer on the presidency. He also said that he had informed Nixon of the break-in and its details as early as September 15, 1972, and that the president had been covering up the incident for more than nine months. The White House had a list of enemies that it kept, Dean testified, and he told the committee that more than seventeen wiretaps had been placed in the homes and offices of White House employees, journalists, and others. Dean revealed that Nixon's reelection committee had engaged in a wide variety of illegal acts, including spying on Senator Edward Kennedy. All three networks carried Dean's five days of testimony.

Though it came down to Dean's word against Nixon's, there was an obvious change in the mood of the country. Doubt grew where support for Nixon had been firmly rooted. The media quickly played on the theme that if Dean were telling the truth, the president of the United States had committed several felonies. Nixon's denials found fewer listeners than before.

Still, the president confided only lies to his new inner circle. In a conversation two weeks later, Nixon told Kissinger and Haig that Dean had not told the truth about the March 21 conversation. "I asked him, I said, 'Now John, is anybody in the White House involved?' He said there's not a scintilla of evidence involving anybody in the White House."[19] The March 21 conversation, in fact, shows that Nixon discussed the cover-up at great length with Dean, telling him that a number of White House aides were involved. Dean advised Nixon that he might need as much as a million dollars to continue the cover-up. Nixon responded that they could get a million dollars. Nixon would never be frank with his new White House subordinates; when it came time to make crucial decisions in late 1973 and in 1974, no one could advise the president, because no one left in the White House knew the whole truth.

Kenneth Clawson, the new director of communications (he retained the title of deputy director until January 1974, but he had taken over the responsibilities of director when Herbert Klein resigned on June 6, 1973), began entertaining reporters and answering their questions informally in meetings at the Old Executive Office Building. Reporters were given drinks and snacks and allowed to fire questions at the former *Washington Post* reporter or other speakers from the administration.[20] Unfortunately for Clawson, White House press relations had deteriorated too far to be rescued by public relations gambits and too much was occurring in the summer of 1973 to be obliterated by snacks and soft drinks. Besides, Nixon's press strategy was always a matter of edicts issued from the inner sanctum of the Oval Office, first under Nixon and Haldeman and then later under Nixon with the usual concurrence of Ziegler. Clawson's efforts with the correspondents held no sway in the pressroom and none in the White House, either. Clawson was proud of his efforts to forge a less tense relationship with the press corps, but he was wasting his time.

Nixon was no fool. He saw where the Watergate investigation was leading, and he knew what would happen if the nature of White House deceit became generally known. Nixon remembered the case of State Department official Alger Hiss, whom Nixon, as a leading member of the House Un-American Activities Committee, had hounded into prison in 1950. Nixon told Dean on April 17: "That son-of-a-bitch Hiss would be free today if he hadn't lied about his espionage. . . . He could have said, 'I—look, I knew Chambers. And, yes, as a young man I was involved with some Communist activities but I broke it off many years ago.' But the son-of-a-bitch lied and he goes to jail for the lie rather than the crime. ... So believe me, don't ever lie with these bastards [investigators]."[21] Nixon's advice reverberated in the Oval Office when Dean testified two months later.

John Mitchell appeared before the Watergate Committee on July 11 and 12, Herbert Kalmbach on July 16, John Ehrlichman for five days beginning on July 24, and H.R. Haldeman for three days beginning on July 30. It was expected that Mitchell's, Haldeman's, and Ehrlichman's testimonies would be the most explosive. Mitchell, in fact, told the committee that the White House had ordered the break-in at Ellsberg's psychiatrist's office and planned a firebombing at the Brookings Institute, among other things. Mitchell maintained that Nixon had not known of these activities. Ehrlichman and Haldeman steadfastly defended the break-ins and buggings as necessary to the security of the government. Haldeman denied that the March 21 conversation with Dean and the president had involved discussions of the cover-up. But these admissions and arguments hardly stirred the waters.

The real surprise testimony came the day that Herbert Kalmbach appeared, but it was Alexander Butterfield, not Kalmbach, who shocked the country and the White House. While government attorneys were interviewing Butterfield on July 13 in anticipation of his appearing before the Watergate Committee, Butterfield mentioned a taped conversation. Prosecutors asked him to explain what he meant, and that is when they learned of the White House taping system.

Butterfield told the Senate Committee and the national television audience on July 16, 1973, that Nixon had been taping most of his conversations for more than two years. Suddenly, the focus of the entire investigation changed. Jerry Landay and Tom Jarriel of ABC were watching the hearings in their West Wing office on the first floor of the White House. "We realized that this nailed it to the wall. Nixon was done," Landay recalled.[22] Here, then, the committee reasoned, was a simple way to resolve the conflict over whether John Dean or the president was lying. The senators simply needed to subpoena the tapes and listen to them. Nixon announced immediately that such a subpoena would violate executive privilege and he would not release them. These battle lines held for nearly a year, but the revelation of the existence of the tapes and the relentless pursuit of those tapes would prove to be Nixon's undoing. The country's business would be frozen for a year, while the economy deteriorated and international relations languished.

Neither the Nixon administration nor the presidency recovered from the Watergate testimony. Shadowy figures who paraded before the Senate Watergate Committee, such as Tony Ulasewicz, the White House sleuth who was paid to gather information on Nixon opponents, and Watergate burglar James McCord, told appalling stories about deceit, domestic espionage, and hush money. Haldeman had been invisible to the public during his tenure as chief of staff and many Americans saw him for the first time during the hearings. This, of course, was after he had resigned from his White House post.

The *New York Times* carried a front-page Watergate story every day except for one during May, June, and July, and 52 percent of the front pages of American newspapers featured Watergate stories covering the days when the committee was in session. Nixon claimed later that he was undone by congressional leaks to the press and unfair and unbalanced media coverage of the Watergate hearings.[23]

Clearly, however, the summer-long testimony of the witnesses and the unflattering inside look at the White House, including Dean's testimony about the list of "White House enemies," subverted Nixon's contention that he was unaware of the details of the scandal and the associated unethical and illegal acts. The testimony also seemed to undercut Nixon's posturing as a victim of the liberal establishment and as a leader who had only tried to protect the interests of the American people. Americans now realized that the Watergate scandal encompassed wholesale domestic espionage and unprincipled campaign tactics. Nixon's claim of martyrdom fell flat. Plus, it was just hard to believe that all those men could be involved, including Nixon's two closest aides, while he remained uninformed about any of it. No matter how the information came out—through testimony or through leaks to reporters—the facts did not change. It was clear that the White House had been riddled by paranoia and disregard for the rights of influential Americans in Washington and elsewhere. And it was becoming ever more obvious that Nixon was involved—up to his neck.

PURSUIT OF THE TAPES

Nixon's refusal to release the tapes brought swift and vociferous reaction from the nation's media. "The White House rationale for making the tapes is that they are for 'posterity,' ultimately to be put in the Nixon Library," editorialized the *Chicago Sun-Times*. "But if they can provide the truth and accuracy of presidential conversations, they should be made public now ... the practice of secret taping and keeping the tapes secret must be added to the lengthening list of unseemly practices of the Nixon administration." Added the *St. Louis Post-Dispatch*: "It might be, we suppose, the easy, proper, and above all politically shrewd tactic for a man who professes to be unfairly and maliciously tormented by his accusers to simply produce the evidence ... it might well also be the most important thing that could be done for the good of the nation whose confidence in government has been badly sapped by the ramifications of the Watergate scandal."[24] Nixon claimed later that he was stunned by the revelation that the tapes existed. "As impossible as it must seem now," he wrote years later, "I had believed that the existence of the White House taping system would never be revealed."[25]

Franklin D. Roosevelt had a secret tape recording device on his desk for several months in 1940 as U.S. entry into World War II approached. Roosevelt suspected that people in his administration would later claim that he covertly led the country to war, so he taped random conversations. Lyndon Johnson had a taping system attached to the White House switchboard and kept recordings from 1964 and 1965 in his possession until his death. Those tapes became public in the 1990s. John F. Kennedy recorded a few conversations, but no president had installed such a complete system as Nixon. Important discussions in all of Nixon's places of work were recorded by the voice-activated system for twenty-eight months, more than 3,500 hours of conversations in all. The existence of such a vast amount of recorded dialogue meant that Nixon's public obfuscations might be unveiled if the tapes became public. President Nixon knew this. Prosecutor Cox knew it. Judge Sirica was aware of it. So was practically everyone else in Washington. Nixon claimed that all conversations came under the rubric of executive privilege—the power to keep items secret—and his last stand against the Watergate avalanche would be this claim of privilege.

The final battle of the Nixon administration was clearly defined by the end of July as a struggle over the tapes. On the popular television show *Sonny and Cher*, the two singers asked their precocious toddler, Chastity, what she would do if she were president of the United States. The audience was led to believe that the question was intended to evoke cute philosophical ruminations. But instead the program's writers had sweet Chastity reply with a smile: "Release the tapes."

Public opinion dipped to heartily skeptical levels. An ABC poll on August 9 revealed that 46 percent of those sampled believed that Nixon was aware of the break-in plans, 55 percent believed that he was aware of the cover-up, and only 29 percent thought he was unaware of either. Respondents didn't think much of the Senate Watergate Committee witnesses either. Only 21 percent believed all or most of what Dean said, Ehrlichman and Haldeman 13 percent each, and Mitchell 10 percent. About 20 percent of the respondents believed none of what the four said.[26]

The president sent a letter to the Senate Watergate Committee on July 26, 1973, rejecting any suggestion of releasing the tapes: "I must respectfully refuse to produce those recordings." Nixon assured the committee that he and his staff would continue to cooperate otherwise. Nixon spoke to the nation by television on August 15, explaining that he would not release the tapes because they might harm the "confidentiality of the presidency." Noting that other witnesses had contradicted Dean, Nixon said he had not learned of the cover-up during the September 15, 1972, conversation, as Dean had claimed. "I said on May 22nd that I had no prior knowledge of the Watergate operation. In all the testimony, there is not the slightest evidence to the contrary. Not a single witness has testified that I had any knowledge of the planning for the Watergate break-in. It is also true, as I said on May 22nd, that I took no part in, and was not aware of, any subsequent efforts to cover up the illegal acts associated with the Watergate break-in."[27] Again, the president was lying, banking on the assumption that the tapes would never become public. The June 23 and September 15 conversations did indeed reveal that he knew of the cover-up, and so did many other recorded discussions. The Watergate noose tightened.

Beyond that, Nixon had to explain why he would take the distasteful step of secretly taping conversations with persons who did not know their private discussions were being recorded. "I think that most Americans do not like the idea of the taping of conversations, and frankly, it is not something that particularly appeals to me," Nixon told a press conference on August 22, his first since March. He added that he had dismantled Johnson's system when he first came to the White House, because he did not approve of such activities. He also claimed that he was being singled out for abuse simply because the existence of his taping system had become known while he was president. Both Johnson and Kennedy had taped White House conversations, he reasoned, so it was just something that was often done.[28]

It was apparent that Watergate questions were beginning to prickle the hair on the back of the president's neck. Thirty minutes into the press conference, he remarked: "I have yet to have ... one question on the business of the people, which shows you how we are consumed with this. I am not criticizing the members of the press, because you naturally are very interested in this issue, but let me tell you, years from now people are going to perhaps be interested in what happened in the world."[29] Nixon was no better a prognosticator than he was a fibber. Later in the press conference, he accused his critics of exploiting Watergate for their own ends: "I would suggest that where the shoe fits, people should wear it. I would think that some political figures, some members of the press perhaps, some members of the television perhaps would exploit it.... There are a great number of people in this country that didn't accept the mandate of 1972. After all, I know that most of the members of the press corps were not enthusiastic—and I understand that—about either my election in '68 or '72."[30]

The Senate hearings and the concurrent furor changed Press Secretary Ronald Ziegler's world, as well as Nixon's. A research memo to Ziegler in July 1973 outlined how drastically the mood of the country and the press had changed. The note revealed empirically how Ziegler was bombarded every day in the summer of 1973 with Watergate questions. The memo revealed that in the months between the day of the break-in, June 17, 1972, and April 17, 1973, in only 33 of 236 press briefings (14 percent) were Watergate or any related topic mentioned. In only 21 briefings (9 percent) was Watergate the dominant subject. The memo noted that Watergate questions had come up in nearly every press briefing after April 17.[31]

On July 23, Nixon rejected requests from both Archibald Cox and the Watergate Committee for copies of the tapes. On August 29, Judge John Sirica ordered Nixon to release selected tapes to be used as evidence in the Watergate grand jury investigation. Nixon's lawyers appealed, and the country dug in for a long court battle.

The stress on Nixon had to be nearly unbearable by the end of August 1973. On August 20, during a trip to New Orleans, Nixon grabbed Ziegler in full view of the correspondents following the president and angrily shoved him toward the reporters, telling Ziegler to deal with them. Nixon later denied he had shoved Ziegler, but the reporting corps agreed it had been nothing less than an angry remonstration. "Helen Thomas [United Press International's chief White House correspondent], an ABC cameraman and I were standing right there," ABC's Jerry Landay said. "Ziegler almost lost his balance. Apparently, Nixon thought that Ziegler was allowing reporters to get too close [physically] to him and he wanted them kept away. Diane Sawyer [a Ziegler aide] came through the plane [Air Force One] later explaining that it had been accidental. Jim Deakin [*St. Louis-Post Dispatch*] and I listened to her politely and when she left, we both gave her the thumbs down."[32] Ironically, that confrontation helped Ziegler. Reporters started to feel sorry for him, and stories appeared detailing the difficult task that the press secretary faced.

Nixon not only feared what the tapes might reveal, but he also resented the incursion on his presidential authority in connection with the tapes. Taping was something he felt that presidents did, and he was not pleased at being singled out just because a special prosecutor felt Watergate superseded the president's right of executive privilege. Besides, Nixon saw Cox as a Kennedy-sympathizing liberal. "Of the eleven senior staff members Cox chose," Nixon wrote in his memoirs, "seven had been associated with John, Bobby, or Ted Kennedy.... The partisan attitude that permeated the top ranks of the Watergate Special Prosecution Force was exceeded by the fervor of the junior members of its staff, most of whom were brash young lawyers intoxicated with their first real taste of power and with the attention being paid to them by a flattering and fawning press."[33]

On September 13, the appellate court ordered Nixon's lawyers and Cox's staff to reach agreement on the tapes. The court would decide on what materials should remain private, if there were materials in dispute. On September 20, the two parties reported to the court that they could not reach agreement on any of the material. Nixon appeared to be winning, but he decided in October to take matters into his own hands.

The months of April, May, June, July, August, and September 1973 were brutal for the beleaguered president. He had heard his own aides and White House operatives reveal some of the most damaging facts about Watergate to date; he had asked his most trusted aides to resign; he had to bear up to intense questioning about secret tapes that he never dreamed the outside world would know about; he read and heard nothing but derogatory reporting about his presidency; and he had to respond to the inquiries of a special prosecutor his own attorney general had appointed and whom he suspected of having Kennedyesque sympathies. All this seemed too much for the president. But if he thought the spring and summer of 1973 had been difficult, he was soon to learn that they would be nothing compared to the turmoil of October.

NOTES

1. Nixon and Colson, Oval Office conversation, January 2, 1973, Nixon Tapes.

2. Nixon, Haldeman, and Ehrlichman, conversation, January 8, 1973, Nixon Tapes.

3. Haldeman, "Talking Paper" to Colson, March 7, 1973, Box 47, Haldeman Papers.

4. Haldeman, personal notes, February 26, 1973, Box 47, Haldeman Papers.

5. H.R. Haldeman, *The Ends of Power* (New York: Times Books, 1978), 181.

6. Haldeman to Dean, memo, March 9, 1973, Box 47, Haldeman Papers.

7. "Statement about Intention to Withdraw the Nomination of L. Patrick Gray III to Be Director of the Federal Bureau of Investigation," April 5, 1973, in *Public Papers of the Presidents: Richard Nixon 1973* (Washington: Government Printing Office, 1973), 257.

8. Haldeman, daily diary, March 25, 1973, entry, Box 47, Haldeman Papers.

9. "Address by the President on Nationwide Radio and Television," April 30, 1973, "President's Remarks and Announcements" file, Box 11, Ziegler Papers; also see "Address to the Nation about the Watergate Investigations," April 30, 1973, *Public Papers of the Presidents 1973*, 328–33.

10. Jerry Landay, interview with author, December 20, 2001.

11. "Remarks at a Republican Fundraising Dinner," May 9, 1973; "Statements about the Watergate Investigations," May 22, 1973, in *Public Papers of the Presidents 1973*, 524, 547–55.

12. Nixon and Ehrlichman, Executive Office Building conversation, April 12, 1973, Nixon Tapes.

13. Nixon and Kissinger, telephone conversation, April 17, 1973, Nixon Tapes; Nixon and Ziegler Executive Office Building conversation, April 27, 1973, Nixon Tapes.

14. Nixon and Ziegler, telephone conversation (from Camp David), May 20, 1973, Nixon Tapes.

15. Richard Nixon, *The Memoirs of Richard Nixon* (New York: Grosset & Dunlap, 1978), 875.

16. Gladys Lang and Kurt Lang, *The Battle for Public Opinion: The President, the Press, and the Polls During Watergate* (New York: Columbia University Press, 1983), 62.

17. Nixon and Ziegler, Oval Office conversation, June 13, 1973, Nixon Tapes.

18. Nixon and Colson, telephone conversation, June 13, 1973, Nixon Tapes.

19. Nixon, Kissinger, and Haig, Oval Office conversation, July 12, 1973, Nixon Tapes.

20. Joseph Spear, *Presidents and the Press: The Nixon Legacy* (Cambridge, Mass.: MIT Press, 1984), 212–13.

21. Nixon and Dean, Oval Office conversation, April 17, 1973, Nixon Tapes.

22. Landay, interview with author, December 20, 2001.

23. Nixon, *The Memoirs of Richard Nixon*, 852–53.

24. *Chicago Sun-Times* editorial, July 19, 1973; *St. Louis Post-Dispatch* editorial, July 19, 1973. Also in roundup of Watergate editorials in "Watergate Files," Box 17, Ziegler Papers.

25. Nixon, *The Memoirs of Richard Nixon*, 900.

26. "ABC Telephone Poll," August 9, 1973, "Watergate Files," Box 17, Ziegler Papers.

27. "Letter Responding to Senate Committee Subpoenas Requiring Production of Presidential Tape Recordings and Documents, July 26, 1973," in *Public Papers of the*

Presidents 1973, 668–69; "Statement by the President, August 15, 1973," and "Statements and Briefings Files," Box 1, Ziegler Papers; also see Stanley I. Kutler, *The Wars of Watergate: The Last Crisis of Richard Nixon* (New York: Knopf, 1990), 384, and "Statement about the Watergate Investigations, August 15, 1973," in *Public Papers of the Presidents 1973*, 698.

28. George W. Johnson (ed.), "Presidential News Conference of August 22, 1973," *The Nixon Presidential Press Conferences* (New York: Earl M. Coleman, 1978), 332–33.

29. Ibid., 339.

30. Ibid., 343.

31. Office memo, "Watergate File," Box 17, Ziegler Papers.

32. Landay, interview, December 20, 2001.

33. Nixon, *The Memoirs of Richard Nixon*, 911.

Chapter 7

Twisting in the Wind

October 1973 brought the whirlwind that eventually swept Richard Nixon from office. A confrontation had been developing since James McCord had changed his mind about remaining silent, and once the prosecutor's demands for evidence turned into a showdown, Nixon was left with few options. But the Watergate investigation was only one part of the misery that washed over the White House that autumn. The world did not stand still while the president resisted Archibald Cox's demands.

The month began with more aggressive pursuit of the tapes. On October 1, Cox subpoenaed a number of recordings of White House conversations, including a June 20, 1972, discussion between Nixon and Chief of Staff H. R. Haldeman. Nixon's choices were to accede to Cox's demands or to continue a public fight in the courts. He decided to negotiate with the Senate Watergate Committee and the court for limited release of the conversations, hoping that Cox would accept the fait accompli once all other parties had approved the compromise. Cox, he knew, wanted access to any relevant tapes and gave every indication that he would not yield. Before a confrontation developed, however, two major events drew Nixon's and the public's attention away from Watergate.

On Saturday, October 6, Syrian and Egyptian forces massed along the Israeli border in preparation for another conflict. Both U.S. and Israeli intelligence at first interpreted the troop movement as routine maneuvers. It was Yom Kippur, the Day of Atonement—the holiest day on the Hebrew calendar when all business activity in Israel was supposed to come to a halt while worshipers gathered in synagogues. The Israeli military was not on high alert. Both intelligence services were wrong. The Arabs meant to fight another war. This time, however, there would be no rapid victory as there had been with the Six-Day War in June 1967.

This fourth conflict in twenty-five years signaled a continuation of failed U.S Middle East policy and a breakdown in U.S. and Israeli intelligence gathering. "I was disappointed by our own intelligence shortcomings, and I was stunned by the failure of Israeli intelligence. They were among the best in the world, and they, too, had been caught off guard," Nixon recalled five years later.[1] Israel sustained heavy losses in the first four days of the war, and on October 9, Nixon ordered the U.S. military to send replacement equipment to the Israelis. Buoyed by the supplies, the Israelis, pushed the Syrians from the Golan Heights and then marched to the outskirts of Damascus, the Syrian capital. The conflict eventually ended on October 22 with a cease-fire arranged by the United States and the Soviet Union. The stalemate convinced Egyptian President Anwar Sadat that further war with Israel was useless. Five years later, Sadat reached a U.S.-brokered peace agreement with Israel's Prime Minister Menachem Begin, ending Egyptian hostilities for the rest of the twentieth century.

A partial Arab oil boycott followed the 1973 war, leaving the United States with a 10 percent reduction in its normal supplies of gasoline. Panic ensued and, for weeks afterward, angry U.S. motorists waited in long lines at service stations. The end of *Pax Americana* had begun, and a generation accustomed to plenty worried about maintaining its comparatively lavish lifestyle. The concern was not unfounded. Americans would see shortages of gasoline and other basic supplies periodically throughout the rest of the decade, and they would suffer from double-digit inflation until the 1980s.

But the surprise war also pointed out a failure within the Nixon administration and previous U.S. administrations throughout the post–World War II period. During the Cold War, the Arabs had turned to both the United States and the Soviets for support and supplies, and then argued that the United States served only Israeli interests. A quarter century after Israel's independence, its neighbors still saw the Jews as intruders. Peace was desired by the Arabs, but only without a sovereign Israel in the region. Consequently, despite decades of U.S. aid and diplomatic overtures to both sides, little had changed since 1948. The policies of the Eisenhower, Kennedy, Johnson, and Nixon administrations had not pacified the Arabs or terminated the constant threat of war. In 1973, Nixon's Watergate problems aggravated these tensions. The Arabs used Soviet support to needle the Americans, and Nixon was in no position to respond forcefully. It may be that the two sides were headed for a fourth war, no matter who was in office in the United States and no matter how U.S. policy was viewed, but Nixon's preoccupation with Watergate had apparently tipped the Arabs away from peace in October 1973, just as Nikita Khrushchev's perception of weakness in John F. Kennedy had led him to order the construction of missile bases in Cuba in October 1962. Secretary of State Henry Kissinger eventually negotiated a truce that would hold until President Jimmy Carter brokered a permanent Egyptian-Israeli agreement, but in 1973 the preoccupation with Watergate appeared to be harming U.S. interests in the Middle East.

Meanwhile, just three days after the Yom Kippur War began, Spiro Agnew walked into Nixon's office and informed the president that he planned to resign the next day. The vice president's bribery case had finally caught up with him. Nixon had been following Agnew's problems closely, and the White House visit came as no surprise. As early as August, news reports had detailed Agnew's growing, legal entanglements. The vice president's response was that he was innocent and was being persecuted by his long-time enemies in the liberal press.[2] But now Agnew had to follow the advice of his lawyers and broker the best deal he could get in court. He pleaded nolo contendere, or no contest—meaning he did not admit the charge but did not deny it either—to one count of income tax evasion in a Baltimore court, was given a three-year suspended sentence, and was fined $10,000. He resigned October 10 as vice president of the United States. According to the tenets of the Twenty-Sixth Amendment to the U.S. Constitution, Nixon was empowered to appoint a new vice president immediately, but that person had to be confirmed by Congress. On October 12, Nixon received permission from House Minority Leader Gerald R. Ford to place Ford's name in nomination. After Senate approval on November 26, the House confirmed Ford on December 6.

Agnew's resignation had great impact, much more so than probably was imagined at the time. A spokesperson for the conservative wing of the Republican Party, the vice president was considered a leading contender for the GOP presidential nomination in 1976, a prospect that, if realized, would put a conservative president into office for the first time in forty-four years. With the press confrontations of the 1968 election campaign and then Agnew's speeches in November 1969, the vice president had attracted the sympathies and adulation of a restive conservative electorate.

This did not impress the White House. Agnew had only been a lightning rod. He was chosen to attack the press because he was considered the most expendable member of the administration. There was irony in Agnew's relationship with Nixon. At the same time that the public saw the vice president as the champion of the beleaguered Nixon White House, Nixon's inner circle privately ridiculed and despised him. While publicly accusing the press of mistreating and misquoting Agnew, Nixon hoped that Agnew's unpopularity among reporters would take some of the heat away from him. This led Nixon to defend Agnew publicly but insincerely. Nixon told the annual convention of the American Society of Newspaper Editors in 1971: "The trouble is he makes news when he hits the press or a golf ball. ... I believe some of his criticisms, if you look at them very objectively, some of the criticisms that he has made in terms of some network coverage and press coverage, you really cannot quarrel with if you examine the whole record. I believe that the vice president's national image of simply being a man who is against a free press, who is against all the press, is just not accurate. ... I defend my vice president."[3] Yet Nixon never consulted Agnew about crucial decisions, and it was clear that he trusted Haldeman and Ehrlichman and later Ziegler and Kissinger much more than he did his vice president. This occurred despite Nixon's favored treatment by Eisenhower when Nixon was vice president and in spite of Nixon's promises to give Agnew a meaningful role in his administration. Now, in a lightning-quick turn of events in October 1973, Agnew was out of politics forever and belatedly the White House realized that Agnew was more valuable to Nixon in office.

His leaving became a political dilemma. Nixon had once referred to Agnew as his insurance policy, meaning that liberals and moderates would not push for a Nixon impeachment or resignation, because that would bring Agnew to the presidency. With Agnew retired, Nixon was naked before his accusers. The possibility of Agnew in the White House would have given pause to even some Republicans, but certainly not a Ford presidency.

The new vice president had represented the Grand Rapids, Michigan, district in Congress since 1949. He was an easygoing, likable politician who had quietly served as minority leader, while higher-profile politicians like Nelson Rockefeller, Richard Nixon, Lyndon Johnson, Hubert Humphrey, George McGovern, and even California Governor Ronald Reagan had positioned themselves for runs at the presidency. Ford's quick confirmation in the Senate reflected both an appreciation of his honesty and integrity and the conviction within the Beltline that Nixon's mounting problems dictated an immediate need for a new vice president to avoid a possible constitutional crisis. Ford realized that there was a good chance that he would be president before 1976, and he kept his distance from Nixon to protect the image of independence.

Meanwhile, the Watergate showdown neared. On October 12 the U.S. Circuit Court of Appeals ruled 5–2 that Nixon had to turn over requested Watergate tapes to District Judge John Sirica, who would review the tapes in private with no one else present. In response, Nixon decided to release edited transcripts of some of the tapes to Sirica and also to the Senate Watergate Committee with Mississippi Senator John Stennis, a Democrat, authenticating the written records. Nixon hoped this would satisfy the court order, but still protect him from wholesale rummaging through the tapes. The details of the Stennis compromise specified that there would be a ban on further subpoenas from Cox's office. All participating parties accepted the concept but Cox, who argued that he would be hamstrung by such diluted evidence if the case went to court. This obstinacy did not sit well with Nixon, so the irate president decided to fire the special prosecutor and return prosecutory jurisdiction over the investigation to the justice department. Attorney General Elliot Richardson worried about the appearance and propriety of such a firing and told Nixon aides that he, Richardson, would have to resign if ordered to dismiss Cox. Richardson must follow his directive, Nixon insisted, because he felt Cox was not following the law but instead acting on his own biases. Nixon reflected later: "Appointing a special prosecutor had been a major mistake, one that I knew would be difficult and costly to remedy." He added that Justice Department "investigators would not have the interest Cox and his staff had in self-perpetuation."[4] Negotiations among White House aides, Richardson, the court, and Cox continued all week.

On the afternoon of Saturday, October 20, Cox brought the impasse to a conclusion by announcing that he would continue to pursue the release of all relevant tapes, thus rejecting the Stennis compromise. Chief of Staff Alexander Haig ordered Richardson to fire Cox. Richardson refused and submitted a public letter of resignation instead. Deputy Attorney General William Ruckelshaus was then asked to fire Cox and, when he refused, he was fired. Solicitor General Robert H. Bork, the third in line in the Justice Department, agreed to dismiss Cox. Thus ended what became known as the "Saturday Night Massacre." Three days later, Bork signed an order abolishing the special prosecutor's office, an order that Nixon surprisingly reversed. Bork reinstated the office on November 2, and Leon Jaworski, a Lyndon Johnson protégé from Texas, was named to replace Cox. Sirica that week asked Nixon's lawyers to comply with the Appellate Court's decision on the Watergate tapes. Having just weathered the furor over Cox's dismissal, Nixon reversed himself and had his lawyers tell Sirica he would provide some of the tapes, while authorizing the continuation of the special prosecutor's office.

ANGRY DISBELIEF

Despite the reversal, public and media denunciation of Nixon was vociferous in the coming week. NBC network anchor John Chancellor labeled the confrontation a crisis. During an interview on October 24, CBS anchor Walter Cronkite asked Cox pointedly, "I wonder whether you agree ... that this whole tape crisis was manipulated to secure your departure." Cox replied that he had no way of knowing. Cox then explained his reasoning for insisting upon the tapes and not accepting edited transcripts: "Maybe summaries will do for a grand jury but, if they won't be accepted by a court, then first I must be assured that I will have the real evidence the court will accept if it comes to a prosecution." He also pointed out that one of Nixon's lawyers told him that Cox would never get the tapes or other evidence of presidential conversations. "And to my way of thinking, it was that that really cut off discussions," Cox added. Later he told Cronkite that the tapes might reveal the "guilt or innocence of Haldeman, Ehrlichman, Mitchell and perhaps others, and second, of course, they would throw light on how much President Nixon knew." Cox clearly indicated that he suspected the tapes could incriminate all parties under investigation, but he also told Cronkite that he didn't think the tapes had been tampered with. The tenor of the interview clearly pointed to Cronkite's skepticism about Nixon's motives.[5] On NBC's *Today Show*, Ruckelshaus reluctantly told interviewer Bill Monroe that Nixon's withholding the tapes to support executive privilege was wrong. "As a rule, I would say that the need at this point to ensure that trials are carried forward probably outweighs that privilege." Ruckelshaus also insisted that he had resigned and had not been fired.[6]

Newspaper editorial writers denounced Nixon, and many newspapers, including some that had supported Nixon, called for his resignation. The *Chicago Sun-Times* labeled Cox's firing a "blunder" and asked if the public could any longer trust the government. "He [Nixon] has put the situation back to square one: the administration conducting an inquiry of itself," the editorial concluded.[7] Syndicated columnists Rowland Evans and Robert Novak wrote: "Although President Nixon's surprise decision to surrender the Watergate tapes after all has abruptly muffled impeachment talk in Congress, there is widespread belief—both in Congress and within the Nixon Administration itself—that he fired Archibald Cox as special prosecutor because Cox was getting too close to unpleasant truths."[8] The staunchly Republican *Chicago Tribune* opined: "It was an almost fatal miscalculation on the president's part to assume that the people of the United States were really on the level when they seemed to say they hold politicians in contempt and venerate statesmen. Actually, they cherish politicians because politicians must pay attention to the people. ... We would hope to see a lot more of Dick Nixon the politician and a lot less of Dick Nixon the statesman."[9] The *New York Times*, the *Atlanta Journal*, the *Denver Post*, and the *Detroit News* all called for Nixon's resignation, as did *Time* magazine in its first editorial in its fifty-year history.

Angry voters drove by the White House honking their horns. Students on college campuses around the nation denounced the president. Clearly, Nixon had miscalculated. The public, dormant after the summer's Watergate hearings, was now aroused once more, and the release of some of the tapes did not wipe away that gut reaction. Nixon knew he was in trouble. "I was taken by surprise by the ferocious intensity of the reaction," Nixon recalled later. "I realized how few people were able to see things from my perspective, how badly frayed the nerves of the American public had become. To the extent that I had not been aware of this situation, my actions were the result of serious miscalculation. But to the extent that it was simply intolerable to continue with Cox as Special Prosecutor, I felt I had no other option than to act as I did."[10]

The House Judiciary Committee held several days of hearings on Cox's dismissal but took no action. Jaworski was instated with the understanding that he could not be removed without tacit approval of the leadership of both parties in Congress. Nixon soon learned that Jaworski could be as tenacious as Cox; the Saturday Night Massacre had aroused anger in all quarters but did little to redirect the battle over the tapes. That same week, stories began to circulate that Nixon's close friend, Bebe Rebozo, had made large illegal contributions to the Nixon campaign the previous year, and Nixon was forced to defend himself once again.

The president responded to the furor by calling a press conference, his second that month. Nixon hoped to keep the televised session focused on the Mideast. He spent the first several minutes of his remarks summarizing the situation there, but his strategy did not work and this turned out to be an ugly press conference. When the president finally turned to Watergate, he tried immediately to put the most positive spin on it. "I can assure you, ladies and gentlemen, all of our listeners tonight [TV and radio audiences], that I have no greater interest than to see that the new special prosecutor has the cooperation from the executive branch and the independence that he needs to bring about that conclusion," he said. Nixon pointed out that every president since Washington had sought to protect the confidentiality of personal records; subliminally Nixon was placing himself in the company of George Washington and Thomas Jefferson.[11]

Reporters' questions drove the press conference in a different direction. Asked by CBS's Dan Rather, a long-time Nixon antagonist, about calls by former Nixon supporters for his impeachment or resignation, the president responded contentiously, "Well, I am glad we don't take the vote of this room let me say." Nixon pointed out that people had been calling for his resignation since his decision to bomb North Vietnam around Christmas a year earlier, linking the calls for impeachment over Cox's firing with presidential decisions that were merely matters of political or ideological inclination.[12]

Still, the press conference had been going reasonably well until Nixon talked about how the press had distorted Vietnam War coverage for years and how news coverage generally was biased. Robert Pierpont of CBS, who had not been nearly as antagonistic to Nixon as Rather had been, asked politely, "Mr. President, you have lambasted the television networks pretty well. Could I ask you, at the risk of reopening an obvious wound, you say after you have put on a lot of heat that you don't blame anyone. I find that a little puzzling. What is it about the television coverage of you in these past weeks and months that has so aroused your anger?" Nixon responded: "Don't get the impression that you arouse my anger." Pierpont answered: "I'm afraid, sir, that I have that impression." Nixon then said: "You see, one can only be angry with those he respects." Nixon later clarified: "Let me say, too, I didn't want to leave an impression with my good friend from CBS over here that I don't respect the reporters. What I was simply saying was this: that when a commentator takes a bit of news and then, with knowledge of what the facts are, distorts it, viciously, I have no respect for that individual."[13]

The reporters in the room got the message, but they were not impressed. Now, they were not afraid of Nixon. He could rage at them all he wanted and still they would only redouble their efforts to tell the public that he was on his way out. They knew he had been badly weakened, and they would not back down. Indeed, each had likely decided that week that he or she had been remiss for quite a while in not asking hard questions of the president and his staff. That would no longer be the case, and all press briefings with Ziegler from that point until August 1974 would be filled with contentiousness, bickering, and accusatory questions. Nixon's war against the press had found a determined counterpart. It would be four months before Nixon met with reporters again, but they would bore in on the president at every opportunity.

On the afternoon of November 15, Haig told Nixon that Nixon's lawyers had been preparing an index of the tapes that were to be turned over to Sirica and that one had a gap. The 18½-minute gap was on a tape with a conversation between Nixon and Haldeman on June 20, 1972. Nixon had known earlier that two other tapes were missing altogether. Those two tapes were of conversations between Nixon and Attorney General John Mitchell on April 1 and June 20, 1972. Nixon's lawyers told Sirica on November 20 about the missing conversations and he announced it to the public. Nixon claimed later that Haldeman's notes on the meeting indicated that they had been talking generally about Watergate but about nothing specific.[14] Haldeman's published diary says only that Nixon worried about the public relations impact of the break-in and that Nixon wanted to change the timing of a press conference so that it didn't look like he was reacting to the arrest of the burglars and the revelation of the break-in. His personal files at the National Archives reflect the same information.[15]

Whatever was said, the revelation of the gap angered Sirica, worried the public, and galvanized the press. Coming so soon after the firing of Cox, the reported gap in the tape hardened attitudes both within Washington and outside the Beltline. The problem worsened when the White House explained that Rose Mary Woods, Nixon's personal secretary, may have accidentally erased the tape while answering the telephone. The evening broadcast of *ABC World News Tonight* on November 15 demonstrated that Woods would have had to have been in a contorted stretching position for several minutes with her finger on the erase button while talking on the telephone in order for the tapes to have been erased accidentally. The White House postulated also that the lamp on her table or her typewriter might have caused the 18½-minute buzz. Neither explanation was credible. "I know that most people think that my inability to explain the 18½-minute gap is the most unbelievable and insulting part of the whole of Watergate. Because of this, I am aware that my treatment of the gap will be looked upon as a touchstone for the candor and credibility of whatever else I write about Watergate," Nixon later reflected. But he insisted that neither he nor Woods had erased the tape purposely and that he did not know how the material had come to be destroyed.[16] Examination of the tape years later showed that it had been erased five or six times, indicating that someone had destroyed the material purposely.

On November 21, a panel appointed jointly by Sirica and the White House examined the tape. Twenty-two days later, Sirica's office released to the news media the panel's conclusions. "Neither the lamp nor the typewriter used by Miss Woods was a likely cause of the 18½-minute buzz on the White House tape of June 20, 1972," the news release said. "Tests made with sophisticated instruments have failed to give any indication that the electric typewriter or the tensor lamp, if used in the arrangement described in the testimony, would have produced the pattern of buzzing sounds on the tape." Nixon told the annual convention of the Associated Press Managing Editors Association in Orlando, Florida, on November 17 that he had known about the missing tapes since the end of September and that the conversations between Mitchell and him had never been taped.[17] It was never learned who erased the June 20, 1972, conversation causing the 18½-minute gap, but thirty years later electronics experts were still trying to figure out what information was on that tape. Rose Mary Woods was never implicated in any wrongdoing. Nixon released seven tapes to Sirica on November 26 and the same tapes to the House Judiciary Committee three months later, but the June 20 conversation was not among those tapes.

The fallout from the Cox firing and the revelation of the gap on the tape had some Nixon advisors suggesting to the president that he should resign, but Nixon repeated for the next nine months that he would not leave his job. Meanwhile, the Internal Revenue Service was looking into some tax claims that Nixon had made years earlier.

The Saturday Night Massacre and the public revelation of the gap on the tape added drama to the scandal, but they were also seemingly clear-cut wrongdoing that the public could understand and relate to. Many a citizen had been fired from a job unfairly and the erasing of a tape had the sinister appearance of someone apparently acting out of desperation. These were not complicated concepts. Nixon lost much of his credibility in the fall of 1973. Thereafter, the public and the media met White House explanations with extreme skepticism.

Because the taping system stopped recording conversations in July 1973, it is not clear what Nixon's logic was in first ordering the firing of Cox, then releasing some of the tapes, and then giving bumbling explanations of the gap in the tape. We have retrospective explanations from Nixon and other principals, who later wrote about their Watergate roles, but those, as we have seen from the evidence, are suspect to hindsight and personal bias. Probably, Haldeman and Ehrlichman could have kept Nixon from making the most obvious mistakes. They would have either placed a better spin on the firing or would have found a way to make Cox the villain. Not only was Nixon losing control of his image and, as Lang and Lang describe, the battle for public opinion, but the president and his advisors also looked inept while it was happening. It is a pity the tapes were still not recording in November. They would have been the only objective sources to tell us what really went on in those frantic days and why a seasoned politician who had been in Washington for most of the previous thirty years could not find a way to explain the mistakes of his administration. Perhaps Nixon was so guilty that he could not find an adequate lie to cover his tracks. Perhaps one lie led to another and another and still another, until the truth could not be distinguished from the falsehood and the perpetrator could only scramble to explain adequately what he could not distinguish himself. Or maybe Nixon was just tired and disoriented.

Part of Nixon's problems, no doubt, related to his inability to find someone who had good advice he would accept. His inner circle consisted of Haig, Kissinger, and Ziegler, none of whom shared Nixon's trust. He had surrounded himself with sycophants for years, not ever looking for someone who would offer anything Nixon did not want to hear (though to the credit of Haig, Kissinger, and Ziegler, the tapes indicate they did offer independent advice occasionally but were not always apprised of the full truth, and Nixon ignored their suggestions anyway). No one could point Nixon in the right direction. Haig, Kissinger, and Ziegler had neither the political acumen nor the president's confidence enough to keep Nixon from blundering. Firing Cox was a serious mistake, and offering unsuitable explanations about the destruction of the June 20, 1972, taped conversation compounded the problem. The presidency had become such a mess that Nixon should have resigned in December 1973, but he was too proud, too stubborn, and too incensed at his perceived enemies to take such a step. So he fought on—needlessly and ineffectively—for another eight months, simply twisting in the wind. On February 25, 1974, he told a news conference: "We have a lot of work left to do, more than three years left to do, and I am going to stay here until I get it done."[18]

In December, Nixon decided not to release any more tapes. On January 4, 1974, he rejected a request from the Senate Watergate Committee to release documents, explaining that "to produce the material you now seek would unquestionably destroy any vestige of confidentiality of Presidential communications, thereby irreparably impairing the constitutional functions of the Office of the Presidency."[19] Jaworski's office geared up to ask for twenty-five more tapes, and in February the House Judiciary Committee requested forty-two tapes. On February 21, aides gave an impeachment report to the Judiciary Committee. The characters had changed somewhat, but the tragic play moved toward the final curtain.

NEW INDICTMENTS

On March 1, 1974, indictments were brought against John Mitchell, H. R. Haldeman, John Ehrlichman, Charles Colson, and three others involved with the Committee to Re-Elect the President. Eighteen days later, James Buckley, the most conservative member of the Senate, called for Nixon's resignation. In May, Barry Goldwater, the conservative senator from Arizona and the 1964 GOP standard-bearer, also suggested that Nixon resign. The argument that the Watergate investigation was merely the invention of liberal antagonists began to disintegrate, and the most influential players in the White House at the time of the Watergate break-in were now charged with felonies.

John Dean faced legal problems of his own. In September 1974 Judge Sirica sentenced him to prison after he pleaded guilty for his role in the Watergate cover-up. Dean served four months and was released in January 1975. Though his prison term was short, it was a depressing time for the former counsel, as it had to have been for all the Watergate figures. "I have no regrets," Dean recalled in 2002. "In all these years, I have never had a negative experience with a person on the street. People still recognize me, if they are old enough." He added that most did not remember him thirty years later because a younger generation knows little about Watergate. Dean returned to college and obtained an accounting degree. He pursued a career in mergers and acquisitions on the

West Coast until the late 1990s, when he began a full-time career as a historian and freelance writer working out of his home in California. "I never planned to make a career of government. I had told Bob Haldeman I was leaving government, but he said I could not leave until after the [1972] election, but I would have left government anyway, Watergate or not. There have been many good things that have happened to me. No regrets."[20]

Nixon turned over eleven more tapes to the House Judiciary Committee in mid-March. During his last presidential press conference, on March 6, 1974, he described the material as "enough material that Mr. Jaworski was able to say that he knew all and that the grand jury had all the information that it needed in order to bring to a conclusion its Watergate investigation."

Helen Thomas, chief White House correspondent for United Press International, asked Nixon, "Mr. Haldeman, your former aide in the White House, has been charged with perjury because he testified that you said it would be wrong to pay hush money to silence the Watergate defendants, and last August you said that was accurate. Can you, and will you, provide proof that you did indeed say it would be wrong?" Nixon answered that he could not comment on pending legal proceedings, but he remembered that he told Dean that money could be raised for the defense of the individuals but not as hush money. He said that after Dean told him that hush money had been paid that he told Dean that was wrong and that the defendants would not be granted clemency.[21] That explanation only convinced the press and the prosecutors that the March 21, 1973, conversation had to be made available to Jaworski and the House Judiciary Committee. Nixon told reporters during the press conference that he would not submit to a cross-examination from prosecutors, because that would weaken the office of the president. Nixon noted years later: "I had to face the fact that we were over a barrel and that my weakened political situation gave the Judiciary Committee license for an unrestrained fishing expedition. I had no practical choice but to comply with their demands. If I refused, they would vote me in contempt of Congress. I made a note on March 22, 1974, at 2 A.M.: 'Lowest day. Contempt equals impeachment.'"[22] But still Nixon fought on.

By April, a majority of the public favored impeachment, according to polls.[23] Nixon reflected on what was happening in the spring of 1974. He noted that the public had not been aware of the specific maneuverings that always go on behind the scenes in the White House. He added: "The American myth that Presidents are always presidential, that they sit in the Oval Office talking in lofty and quotable phrases, will probably never die—and probably never should, because it reflects an important aspect of the American character. But the reality of politics and power in the White House is very different."[24] Nixon, of course, was trotting out the old argument: he was only doing what every other president did on the sly. Perhaps that is true, but he was more blatant and clumsier about it. He was wrong, too, that the American people would always see the president as a man who spoke in lofty phrases and was high minded. That had been the case for decades, perhaps since the time of Theodore Roosevelt, but that popular sentiment surely died after Watergate.

In May the *Chicago Tribune* called for Nixon's resignation, and so did seven other prominent newspapers. On April 29, in a televised address to the nation, Nixon had promised to release transcripts of the tapes, but that material turned out to be fragmented and useless.

Meanwhile, Bob Woodward and Carl Bernstein, the two *Washington Post* reporters who had disappeared from the spotlight in December 1972, reemerged in June 1974 with the publication of their book, *All the President's Men*, which recorded their experiences in uncovering details of the early Watergate investigation. The book was a runaway best-seller, and suddenly Nixon's two antagonists were national heroes. In the book, the two reporters pointed out frequently that they had pursued the Watergate investigation vigorously while no other reporter in Washington had shown interest in the scandal. This stung the Washington press corps, which bore in on Nixon in the summer of 1974.

On April 16, Jaworski subpoenaed sixty-four additional tapes, a move that was opposed by Nixon's lawyers. On May 31, Sirica sided with the prosecutor and ordered the tapes be released. An appeal of that order reached the U.S. Supreme Court in July. Nixon stopped meeting with reporters, and Ziegler's press briefings became so heated that someone else frequently took his place so that he would not have to deal with the strain daily.

In May, the House Judiciary Committee, under the chairmanship of Democrat Peter Rodino, began impeachment hearings. This step gave pause to a large segment of the public and to many in the media. In 185 years, no live president had ever left before the end of his term. Andrew Johnson's impeachment in 1868 had come to be seen as the political vendetta that it was, and so he was not convicted by the Senate and removed. Was Nixon so wrong that he deserved that stigma? Had not the country been through enough? What would be the harm in waiting another twenty-nine months and simply letting Nixon serve out his term? If Nixon would only release the tapes that showed that he had been an innocent bystander, then the guilty could be punished and the president could limp through the next two years. Once the Judiciary Committee began to collect information, however, the committee would either have to publicly back down or adopt articles of impeachment.

At first, most observers figured that the committee would simply sidestep the issue. After all, it had been Cox who pursued unaltered versions of the tapes. The Senate Watergate Committee and even Sirica had been willing to accept edited versions from Nixon, through the Stennis compromise. The Judiciary Committee was expected to back down when a showdown came.

Kissinger negotiated a tentative agreement in the Middle East, and in June Nixon flew to Egypt to cement the pact. Nixon also visited Syria, Saudi Arabia, Israel, and Jordan. He then traveled to the Soviet Union to meet with Leonid Brezhnev before vacationing in San Clemente, California, for two weeks. "When we traveled with Nixon, people in the crowds spat on us," former ABC reporter Jerry Landay remembered. "When we traveled to California that summer, someone in the crowd demanded of me, 'Is it really that bad in Washington?' I looked at him and I said, 'It's worse,' but you could tell he didn't believe me."[25] The public may have finally accepted part of the truth about Nixon, but many were just upset with the reporters who brought them the bad news. When Nixon finally returned to Washington for good, he found that the atmosphere was as hot in the capital as it had been in the desert by the pyramids.

Nixon's attorney, Fred St. Clair, appeared before the committee in late June and submitted a partial transcript of a tape the committee had been seeking for months. Clearly, the Nixon administration was toying with the committee. On June 27, committee chair Rodino told reporters that he thought that all the twenty-seven Democrats of the thirty-eight-member Judiciary Committee would vote for impeachment.[26] The Judiciary Committee listened to testimony from some of the Watergate characters such as Colson and Butterfield.

On July 24, the U.S. Supreme Court ruled unanimously that Nixon would have to release the tapes that were requested by Sirica, upholding the decision of the Appellate Court and rejecting Nixon's claims of executive privilege. Nixon would have to release damning material, including the June 23, 1972, tape in which he ordered that the CIA be used to block the FBI Watergate investigation.

Three days later before Nixon released any of the new tapes, the Judiciary Committee adopted its first article of impeachment, 27-11, on the charge that Nixon had obstructed justice. The second article, passed on July 29, charged that Nixon had abused his power as president, and the third impeachment article, passed on July 30, alleged that Nixon had impeached himself by refusing to release the tapes to the Judiciary Committee. The three articles were sent to the House floor for debate scheduled to begin on August 19.

Woodward and Bernstein wrote another book a year later about how Nixon reacted to the public outcry for his resignation. The book, *The Final Days*, depicts Nixon as nearly suicidal, crying like a baby and seeking salvation, while asking Kissinger to pray with him. Obviously, since only Kissinger was in the room with Nixon, it is apparent that Kissinger had talked with the two reporters later. Kissinger did not deny the depictions. Nixon's portrayal of his final days was much more dignified. He claimed to have told Haig on August 8 that he had decided to resign on August 1, eight days before his actual resignation.

There was great fear in Washington that Nixon would somehow place the nation in danger while deciding his own fate; he might order a military attack. The military was on high alert. This, of course, did not occur. Nixon simply charted what might happen if he did release the tapes, and his calculations were that he could not explain away some of the conversations that would be made public, particularly the June 23, 1972, discussion. A number of Washington reporters, including ABC's Landay, said that Nixon drank heavily in those days and that he often slurred his words when he spoke on television or to reporters.

On August 5, Nixon decided to release the June 23 tape with a written explanation that the tape was of a private conversation that was never to have been made public. He added that it sounded much worse than what had actually been meant. The public and the Congress did not agree. The din in Washington was deafening.

The next day, Nixon met with his entire Cabinet and asked the members to go on with their work as best they could. He thanked them for their industriousness and, without saying as much, clearly indicated that he was going to resign. Nixon then began work on his resignation speech. Most of his supporters on the Judiciary Committee had publicly abandoned him after the "smoking gun" tape was released. Nixon had only two choices: he could continue to fight to remain in office and be impeached, probably before the end of the year, or he could spare himself and the country further turmoil by submitting his resignation. He chose the latter.

During the press briefing of August 8, Ziegler announced that Nixon would address the nation that night. Speculation had been frenzied for three days since the release of the tape and it was widely reported that Nixon would announce his resignation. This was Ziegler's last briefing. Jerald terHorst, Ford's new press secretary, would take over those chores, and Ziegler, the youngest person ever to serve as a press secretary in the White House, would become a footnote. There was a somber and disquieting mood in the pressroom. While nearly all the correspondents had felt for quite a while that impeachment was the only alternative, it was nevertheless unnerving to know that the president was actually about to leave office. No one wanted to appear to be kicking Nixon while he was down and no one wanted to seem gleeful about such an American tragedy. It was time to just drag through the last horrible day of a nightmarish administration that had taken a mental and physical toll on every reporter assigned to cover the story. Most could hardly remember a press conference or press briefing that would be considered "normal." Turmoil and contentiousness between press and president had become so common and so matter-of-fact that any change in direction would be a welcome relief. But for the moment there was one more Nixon story to cover.

That night, Nixon prepared to appear on television as a huge audience in the United States and around the world tuned in. "We were all gathered in the first floor West Wing. It was a hot night, stifling," Landay recalled. "The air conditioning couldn't keep up because there were a mob of reporters in there. The doors and windows were locked in the pressroom. We were seriously talking about some kind of coup where Nixon would stay in office illegally. I called over to the White House police office and asked why we were locked in. He said, 'The old man wants to take one last walk around the grounds without being accosted by the press.' My own sense was that that was just the last shot over the bow at the press he had hated so intensely [keeping them in uncomfortable quarters]."[27] When the broadcast began, Nixon said that he still did not want to resign, that he was not a quitter, and that resigning was anathema to everything he believed in. "To continue to fight through the months ahead for my personal vindication would almost totally absorb the time and attention of both the President and the Congress in a period when our entire focus should be on the great issues of peace abroad and prosperity without inflation at home. Therefore, I shall resign the Presidency effective at noon tomorrow," Nixon said.[28]

On August 9, 1974, he gathered his family about him on the podium, talked about how wonderful his late mother and father had been, and wished everyone in the White House well. "And so, we leave with high hopes, in good spirits, and with deep humility, and with very much gratefulness in our hearts," Nixon added.[29] Then he and Patricia Nixon boarded a helicopter waiting on the White House lawn. The helicopter took him to Andrews Air Force Base, from which he flew to his home in San Clemente. A cheering throng met him in California, and he waved and smiled before disappearing from public view for several years. Gerald Ford was sworn in as the thirty-eighth president of the United States, the only person ever to occupy the office without having been elected to the office of either the vice president or president. Ford's attitudes and ideas would be a welcome change from Nixon's, and for the first month of his presidency things actually did seem to be normal in Washington.

Nixon had done the "right" thing, but Washington was emotionally drained and the government's attitude toward both the public and reporters would not be soon forgotten. Watergate was not about a break-in; it was about a mindset and that mindset had now been revealed publicly. Nixon's claim that his behavior was only typical of how presidents actually behaved in private was a chilling disappointment to the American people. His leaving office did not change that. Indeed, the real tragedy of Watergate was not the resignation of the president or the revelation of misdeeds at the highest level of the executive branch of government, but the aftermath that would change public perceptions for the foreseeable future and alter the relationship between the press and the president for much of the remainder of the century. The real Watergate disaster was only beginning in August 1974.

NOTES

1. Richard Nixon, *The Memoirs of Richard Nixon* (New York: Grosset & Dunlap, 1978), 920.

2. Stanley I. Kutler, *The Wars of Watergate: The Last Crisis of Richard Nixon* (New York: Alfred A. Knopf, 1990), 391–93.

3. "Panel Interview at the Annual Convention of the American Society of Newspaper Editors," April 16, 1971, in *Public Papers of the Presidents of the United States: Richard Nixon* (Washington: Government Printing Office, 1972), 548–49.

4. Nixon, *The Memoirs of Richard Nixon*, 929.

5. Transcript of Walter Cronkite CBS interview with Archibald Cox, October 24, 1973, "Tapes—Watergate" file, Box 15, Ziegler Papers.

6. NBC *Today Show*, Bill Monroe interview with William Ruckelshaus, October 22, 1973, 3, "Tapes—Watergate" file, Box 15, Ziegler Papers.

7. *Chicago Sun-Times* editorial, October 24, 1973.

8. Rowland Evans and Robert Novak, syndicated column, October 24, 1973, "Tapes—Watergate" file, Box 15, Ziegler Papers.

9. *Chicago Tribune* editorial, October 25, 1973.

10. Nixon, *The Memoirs of Richard Nixon*, 937–38.

11. "Press Conference No. 35, President of the United States," October 26, 1973, Box 13, Ziegler Papers, 3–4; also see "The President's News Conference of October 26, 1973" in George W. Johnson (ed.), *The Nixon Presidential Press Conferences* (New York: Earl M. Coleman, 1978), 366.

12. Ibid., 368.

13. Ibid., 373.

14. Nixon, *The Memoirs of Richard Nixon*, 949.

15. H. R. Haldeman, *The Haldeman Diaries: Inside the Nixon White House* (New York: G. P. Putnam's Sons, 1994), June 20, 1972, entry, 473; Haldeman Diary entry, June 20, 1972, Box 47, Haldeman Papers.

16. Nixon, *The Memoirs of Richard Nixon*, 950.

17. Press release of December 13, 1973, from Sirica Court, "Tapes—Watergate" file, Box 15, Ziegler Papers; "Question-and-Answer Session at the Annual Convention of the Associated Press Managing Editors Association, Orlando, Florida, November 17, 1973" in *Public Papers of the Presidents 1973*, 947–48.

18. Johnson, *The Nixon Presidential Press Conferences*, "The President's News Conference of February 25, 1974," 383.

19. "Letter to the Chairman of the Senate Select Committee on Presidential Campaign Activities Responding to Subpoenas Requiring Production of Presidential Tape Recordings and Documents, January 4, 1974," in *Public Papers of the Presidents 1974* (Washington: Government Printing Office, 1975), 5.

20. John Dean interview with the author, January 15, 2002.

21. Johnson, *The Nixon Presidential Press Conferences*, "The President's News Conference of March 6, 1974, 386–87.

22. Nixon, *The Memoirs of Richard Nixon*, 993.

23. Ibid., 994.

24. Ibid., 996.

25. Jerry Landay, interview with author, December 20, 2001.

26. Kutler, *The Wars of Watergate*, 490.

27. Landay, interview with author, December 20, 2001.

28. "Address to the Nation Announcing Decision to Resign the Office of the President of the United States," in *Public Papers of the Presidents 1974*, 626.

29. "Remarks on Departure from the White House, August 9, 1974," in *Public Papers of the Presidents 1974*, 631–32.

Chapter 8

After the Resignation

But I have followed, as you have, the press briefings by Mr. Ziegler. His job
is difficult because he must serve two masters: He must serve the President
of the United States, and he must serve the press. He must serve each with
equal loyalty and devotion.

Richard Nixon to reporters, April 14, 1973[1]

As with many public statements by Richard Nixon, there was no truth to what
he told White House correspondents in 1973. Nixon saw Ronald Ziegler as
strictly a mouthpiece for Nixon's ideas and attitudes. Ziegler had no independence whatsoever, and by the time Nixon resigned, the office of the press secretary had been badly damaged. "Ziegler did only what he had to do," presidential
counsel John Dean recalled thirty years later. "Ziegler just came in every day
and got his instructions and he did whatever the president wanted, including
sometimes playing games with the press."[2] Whether the destruction of the office of press secretary would be permanent was still an open question. Gerald
Ford had it within his power to restore to that office the prestige that had existed during John F. Kennedy's presidency. Ford attempted to do so, but in the
end he failed miserably. After 1974, it was difficult for any press secretary to
gain a decent relationship with reporters. Eventually, the image and purpose of
the office changed drastically.

This was but one of many short-term and long-term problems that followed
the Nixon administration and the Watergate scandal. One immediate problem
in the summer of 1974 dominated the rest and led to a public review of the
press secretary's role. In August and into September Ford wrestled with what
to do about Nixon's culpability in the Watergate cover-up. A comprehensive
pardon might put the Watergate mess behind the country once and for all, but

it also might stir passions needlessly on Capitol Hill and throughout the nation again.

Ford had named Jerald terHorst, Washington bureau chief of the *Detroit News*, as his press secretary. During the first month of the Ford administration, terHorst had lowered the emotional temperature in the press offices in the West Wing and basement of the White House, though reporters wondered about Ford's credentials. "We had the sense that Jerry Ford had not proved himself. There was skepticism about whether he had the feet to fill the boots [of the presidency]," recalled Jerry Landay, then an ABC White House correspondent.[3] Nevertheless, there was a much more congenial atmosphere in the pressroom, and terHorst, who had been one of the regular correspondents, seemed to have the elixir to wipe away the mistrust. He was close to Ford, too, and because he obviously enjoyed Ford's confidence, his presence in the briefing room seemed to put to rest whatever suspicions reporters had about Ford's motives. This then was to be the return to the era of good feelings in the West Wing, the type of atmosphere that had existed before Vietnam and Watergate.

But on Saturday, September 7, Ford called terHorst into his office and told him that he was going to extend to Nixon a full pardon, even before Nixon had been charged with any crime. Ford had informed reporters only a few days before that he had not made any decision about blanket absolution for his predecessor. Apparently, terHorst was not as close to Ford as had been perceived, because he had no hint of Ford's intentions until about twelve hours before Ford was to make the announcement. The surprised press secretary told Ford that he emphatically disagreed, so much so that he candidly added that he would resign if Ford took such a step. The public outcry over a pardon would be thunderous, and Ford would destroy all the good will that had accumulated over the last month, terHorst counseled. The president considered terHorst's advice and threat but decided to go ahead with the pardon anyway. He announced his decision on Sunday, September 8, 1974. Overwhelming reaction made Ford realize that he had underestimated the impact of the pardon and that terHorst had been right.

Pundits from every part of the country lambasted Ford. Persons accused of crimes both great and small all across the nation demanded pardons. Reporters interviewed opposition politicians who used the occasion to piously decry the unfairness of such a gesture. Privately, they looked enthusiastically toward the 1974 off-year congressional elections. Ford's approval rating in public opinion polls dropped precipitously. Some speculated that Ford and Nixon had arranged a bargain before Nixon resigned. It was immaterial that Ford had acted out of conscience and that he felt Watergate was a disease that had to be eliminated in order for the country to become healthy again. The new president paid the price of his move during the remainder of his 29-month term. Whatever legislative proposal Ford set forth, whatever public appearance he made, and whatever foreign policy initiatives he undertook from that point forward, he was seen as politically inept and unqualified, and sometimes he was even ridiculed. As Landay suggested, this was the initial inclination of journalists. The pardon only convinced them that they were right in their first assessments.

Some historians and political scientists have come to regard the pardon in a different light. The John F. Kennedy Library and Foundation in May 2001 honored Ford as the recipient of the Kennedy Profile in Courage Award. The honor is bestowed annually upon an elected official who has "withstood strong opposition from constituents, powerful interest groups, or adversaries to follow what she or he believes is the right course of action." The award was named after the Pulitzer Prize–winning book written by Kennedy and published in 1957. *Profiles in Courage* recounts the stories of eight U.S. senators who risked their careers to fight for what they believed in. Ford received the achievement icon from Kennedy's lone surviving family member, daughter Caroline Kennedy. "For more than a quarter century, Gerald Ford proved to the people of Michigan, the Congress, and our nation that politics can be a noble profession," she said. "As President, he made a controversial decision of conscience to pardon former President Nixon and end the national trauma of Watergate. In doing so, he placed his love of country ahead of his own political future."[4] Obviously, the Kennedy Library and Foundation is not a bastion of conservative Republican politics, and the honor suggests an extraordinary act of bipartisanship.

Ford lost the 1976 presidential election to political neophyte Jimmy Carter, the governor of Georgia, and he almost lost the Republican nomination to former California Governor Ronald Reagan. He would have been the first incumbent president to be denied his party's nomination in almost one hundred years. Was the pardon an act of courage, or was it a political blunder by a politician who could not see what a disaster he was creating for himself and his party? Probably, the truth lies somewhere in between. Ford could have waited a year or so to see how the Nixon prosecution wended its way through the system. Perhaps the special prosecutor's office (Jaworski had resigned by then) would not have prosecuted Nixon, or perhaps the courts would have seen fit not to allow the case to be heard. Ford wanted Watergate over with but the pardon had just the opposite effect, which he should have been able to foresee after having served twenty-four years in Congress. Watergate dominated the public consciousness for several more years, and the nation's "long national nightmare" was not over. As an act of courage, it is to be greatly admired; as a political tactic, it was the one of the most inept gestures of the twentieth century. Perhaps, twenty-five years later, some who did not live through the era or who were not students of politics at the time could see in hindsight that Ford's interest in healing wounds outweighed the anger of the time. That is the advantage of historical retrospect, but it does not show much perception of the moods of Washington and the country in 1974.

Yet, an ancillary side effect from the pardon kept the presidency and the press at odds and perhaps had as much influence on the future of the press-president-public relationship as the political turmoil. Not only did the press corps regard the Ford White House with skepticism and general contempt after September 8,

1974, but the correspondents also remained suspicious of the office of press secretary. Ron Nessen, an NBC White House correspondent, took terHorst's place, but he did not have terHorst's deft manner. TerHorst's resignation was a signal to the correspondents that White House press relations had not changed from Nixon's administration to Ford's. As Nixon said, but did not mean, in his remarks to correspondents in April 1973, a press secretary is supposed to serve two masters. TerHorst took that perception to heart and quit when he was asked to serve only one. After Ford was defeated in 1976, no president for the remainder of the century appointed a working journalist as press secretary, and the role of the press office changed immeasurably. No president after Ford ever claimed with any conviction that a press secretary served two roles.

Nixon accepted the pardon and stayed away from reporters and television cameras. Stories began to circulate about sightings of Nixon walking along the beach near his San Clemente home, a solitary figure who was to be pitied and even perhaps admired. The Watergate characters who surrounded him during his first term served short prison sentences. Most wrote their memoirs, and several of these books made the New York Times best-seller list. They told their stories from their own perspectives, of course, placing themselves in the best light possible. Charles Colson experienced a religious rebirth just before entering a federal penitentiary and became a devout Christian. H. R. Haldeman, John Ehrlichman, John Dean, John Mitchell, E. Howard Hunt, G. Gordon Liddy, and eighteen others served prison time. Ehrlichman claimed that Dan Rather dogged him for the rest of his life, making certain that people remembered his role; Rather has denied the charge. Both Ehrlichman and Colson denounced Dean. Haldeman speculated in his book that Nixon authorized the Watergate burglary, but Haldeman's speculations hold little credibility. Few of Nixon's former associates had much connection with him again after he left office. Nixon, Ehrlichman, and Haldeman died in the 1990s.

In retrospect and in answer to one of the questions posed in the introduction, it was Nixon and Haldeman who authorized and approved the intelligence-gathering campaigns against journalists and political opponents. It was probably Nixon, under Haldeman's advice, who approved the Watergate break-in. It was certainly Nixon, Haldeman, and Ehrlichman who created the atmosphere in the White House that led to wholesale violations of individual privacy and civil rights of anyone who was perceived as a White House enemy. The spying and the covert activities began within weeks of Nixon's taking office and continued until the spring of 1973. Nixon did not react to hostile acts by reporters and political enemies; he and his staff took the underhanded fight to them before they had time to wipe the inaugural confetti from their shoes. The spying on reporters and political opponents began within three months of Nixon taking office. The enemies list was such a cause célèbre because it seemed to fit the Nixon White House scheme so well. It wasn't a meaningless list of names, but a reflection of the loathing and paranoia that mirrored the inner circle from the time Nixon took office.

"Watergate" was a series of step-by-step covert and overt activities that lasted for almost the entire Nixon presidency. The subterfuge and the verbal attacks on Nixon's political opponents and the press became more bold and reckless as the first term of his administration progressed. Eventually, totally unprincipled and careless figures such as Hunt and Liddy were given far too much latitude. The obsessive spying and money laundering became almost a vaudeville comedy, and in June 1972 the White House got caught. But it wasn't the break-in or the slush funds or the cover-up or the tapes that destroyed Richard Nixon. It was the White House mindset that tolerated such unconscionable and insipid acts. As Colson said in January 1973, the problem was the logic that drove someone to tell the burglars to "do it."

It was a shame that the president chose such a path during his six years in office. Many argue that the Nixon presidency was partially a success. He opened relations with China, ended the U.S. involvement in the Vietnam War, promoted social welfare programs for the poor, and allowed civil rights progress to continued. "He obviously had things that he did well," Dean observed. "His grasp of world affairs, and his knowledge of them is probably unmatched. He didn't have much interest in domestic affairs, which resulted in somewhat moderate, if not in some instances, liberal policies that got implemented."[5] Throw out Watergate, and the Nixon presidency would be considered a rousing success. Of course, we can't ignore Watergate, because it was more than just "a third-rate burglary," as Ziegler described it. It was a lesion on the surface that revealed a malignancy below.

Nixon preoccupied himself and his staff with concerns over how he was reflected in the nation's media. This obsession left little time to deal adequately with affairs of state. Agnew's speeches in 1969, the fuss over the 1971 CBS television documentary "The Selling of the Pentagon," the 1971 Pentagon Papers confrontation, and the covert activity during the 1972 election campaign all were symptoms of the White House's obsession with the press and political opponents. The tapes released in 1996 clearly trace the White House's daily infatuation with Washington reporting and with liberals generally.

Such concerns were always integral portions of the modern presidency. Presidents both great and mediocre worried about the message that the media sent the public and who would be standing in the way of policy initiatives and reelection. Most tolerated reporters and the loyal opposition while concentrating on their administrative duties and, hoping that, if they succeeded in the responsibilities, media coverage would take care of itself. Herbert Hoover, who ran a media-savvy election campaign in 1928, became so introverted and uncommunicative during the latter years of his depression-era presidency that he failed to capitalize on potential media bonanzas when they presented themselves and left reporters to concentrate on his failures. Unlike Nixon, Hoover just didn't care what reporters were saying as he sought reelection in 1932. Most presidents did spend time polishing their images, but at a certain point they turned to the duties of the office and let press matters take care of themselves. They knew when to be statesmanlike and when to be politicians. Contrary to the opinion of the *Chicago Tribune* in 1973, Americans do like their leaders to be statesman-like. If there is a lesson from the Nixon era, it is that Nixon simply forgot how to be a national and international leader.

That is too bad, because such an inspirational head of state was what Americans needed in the 1970s. Nixon had promised to bring Americans together and, plagued by war and domestic turmoil, most Americans desperately wanted and needed that to happen. Americans emerged from the 1960s fearful and uncertain. The 1960s had been a time of questioning of values, and most Americans, not just conservatives, wanted the questioning to stop. They wanted a return to basic values. Nixon's silent majority was not a fiction. The nation's turn to the right politically after Nixon left office is clear testimony as to how Americans wanted the political process to serve them.

But in addition to the historical chain of events, the 1970s were marked by television's rise in power and influence. National evening newscasts had become so important in Washington politics that the presidency became a stage set for the three networks. Nixon's obsession with media was partly justified because of the changing role of television in the daily lives of Americans. He, more than any other president, did have to find an accommodation with a visual medium that often took on a life of its own.

From the time of Theodore Roosevelt (1901–1909), presidents had developed organized and somewhat orderly relationships with the Washington press corps and the nation's media owners and managers. For most of the seventy years between Theodore Roosevelt's time and Richard Nixon's era, the president controlled the media. He and his press secretary released information when they wished it to be circulated generally, they punished reporters who were critical or wrote negative stories too often, and they fashioned relationships with the media that clearly placed the president in a dominant position. Kennedy could pick up the telephone and ask the *New York Times* to sit on a story about the Bay of Pigs. Harry S Truman could ban some reporters from pleasure trips aboard his presidential yacht, if he disliked them enough, and invite other correspondents on such outings, if they were not as critical of him. Franklin D. Roosevelt held press conferences in the Oval Office and placed the more critical reporters in the back of the room, where they could hardly hear the discussions. Sometimes Roosevelt even dressed them down in front of their colleagues, if he found their stories or columns unacceptable.

That is partly why incumbency, especially in the White House, became such a powerful tool for officeholders in the twentieth century. Media attention at all levels of political office gave the incumbent a tremendous boost. Only three presidents held office between 1933 and 1961, the fewest three-decade changes in the history of the presidency. Between 1901 and 1972 only two presidents were defeated in office, and that was because of a split in the Republican Party (William Howard Taft in 1912) and the country's most disastrous economic downturn (Herbert Hoover in 1932). In the eighteen years following Nixon's resignation, three more presidents were defeated, clearly indicating a change in the advantage of incumbency. Certainly, television's influence had much to do with this lack of power. Americans could see the presidency up close on their screens. In many cases, they relied on what they saw and heard on television to make up their minds about where the nation was positioned in the world and what the president stood for. This wasn't only because of television's presentation of the news or because of unfair commentary; it was just the nature of pictures and images on television. The Vietnam War and the images it created were clear examples of how events could take on lives of their own through television. The incumbent could not control his image as well as his predecessors had in the first seventy years of the twentieth century. Nixon far overreacted to this shift. Instead of accepting the changed role of media as one of the quirks of destiny, Nixon brooded about it and plotted against an amorphous monster that he could never defeat.

Mostly, this was a reflection of a flaw in Nixon's personality. From his earliest days, Nixon brooded about his relationship to the elite, whether it was his dislike for richer kids who did not have to work in their fathers' grocery stores after school or whether it was for his political opponents and media moguls who, he felt, helped to bring about his defeat in the 1960 election. Nixon did not know how to live and let live. He *had* to strike out at those who made his life uncomfortable. In that sense, he was simply not qualified to be president, no matter how insightful he was on foreign affairs and no matter how adroit he was in handling the political process.

What of Nixon's claims that the media had a liberal bias and so were unfair to him? That is complicated, but one thing can be argued for certain: Nixon certainly was more unfair to correspondents in the White House than they were to him. As to the liberal bias, media do not have a common chain of command. News organizations compete with one another. Too often in Washington they follow each other's stories and show too little initiative, but this has nothing to do with ideology. The *New York Times, Washington Post,* and *Los Angeles Times* had liberal editorial policies in the 1970s and later (the *Los Angeles Times* was purchased by the Chicago Tribune Company in 2000, and the extent of its liberal leanings remained to be determined in the early years of that decade), but the wire services, the national newsmagazines, and most newspapers could not be considered generally liberal. Reporting on network television is too tepid to be considered liberal or conservative. Jimmy Carter, a moderate Democrat, was highly critical of the media in Washington, claiming that he never received the benefit of the doubt or a fair hearing. In the 1990s, the media spent an inordinate amount of time following liberal President Bill Clinton's sex scandals, and he, too, found great fault with media emphases.

While assessing the news stories in the media that are obviously liberal, one cannot assume that ideology always drives coverage. Reporters seek stories. Columnists, commentators, and editorial writers provide ideological opinion. A blanket charge that the media are "liberal" in their coverage is to misunderstand the nature of journalism and what a reporter is empowered to do. The notions about journalism in the 1930s that persuaded *Chicago Tribune* editor and publisher Robert R. McCormick to send reporters out to find negative stories about Franklin D. Roosevelt were not the same as the concept of news reporting that existed during and after Nixon's time. If anything, the media in the 1970s, 1980s, and 1990s became more ideologically neutral because corporate owners were more concerned about earning profits than pushing political agendas. More than 30 percent of daily newspapers did not even endorse candidates in presidential elections in the 1990s, so as not to offend one set of readers or another. That is not to say that New York, being the center of national reporting does not tilt news coverage to an East Coast bias, but the charge of "a liberal" media is hard to accept.

The national networks backed down for a time after Agnew's initial criticisms in late 1969. They were afraid of Nixon and his people. Only when the White House inner circle made the attacks personal and became unreasonable in their demands, particularly over the CBS documentary "The Selling of the Pentagon," did the networks fight back. The charge of liberalness was merely a ploy for Nixon and his people to regain control over what the nation's media reported. It worked only for a short time. Ironically, it became a siren's song for conservatives who repeated the charge for more than thirty years after Agnew first aired such complaints. That the charge was largely baseless in the first place seemed to have no particular importance. Such an insinuation remained a rallying cry with people disaffected by national and international events and by those innately distrustful of media and reporters in the first place.

IMAGE POLISHING

After he resigned, Nixon felt throughout the remainder of his life that he could improve his place in history if he could only convince the public to see the world of 1969 to 1974 his way. After all, many presidents have increased greatly in stature after leaving office. Abraham Lincoln, who was reviled by critics both North and South during his lifetime, has become nearly a god to many Americans, even some historians. Theodore Roosevelt's image waxed and waned throughout the twentieth century as historians emphasized first his record on trust-busting and then later his jingoistic acts of international intrigue, including the shabby way in which America gained control of the Panama Canal Zone. Harry Truman saw his approval ratings plunge to record post–World War II levels in the early years of the Cold War, but he was remembered fondly in the twenty-first century as "Give-'em-hell Harry." Even Lyndon Johnson, despised by conservatives who decried his "wasteful" spending and by liberals who deplored his military decisions in Vietnam, is regarded a generation later as one of the ten best presidents of all time. These are only a few examples of how presidents were seen differently in the years after they left office. Nixon emerged from his three years of self-imposed exile to claim his place in history.

Within two weeks of leaving office, Nixon asked for memos from his staff to begin planning how to refurbish his image.[6] Later, he offered commentary on the events of the day, seemingly candid observation that provided good stories for reporters. He traveled to foreign countries, where he had triumphed with successful policy decisions, and where the events of Watergate were seen as murky political conundrums.

In 1977, the former president agreed to a series of broadcast interviews with David Frost, a talk-show host. Then Nixon published his memoirs a year later. Both were long-anticipated media events, but each was a disappointment. Nixon stuck by his story about his not knowing of the break-in or the cover-up of Watergate and related covert activities until his March 21, 1973, conversation with John Dean in the Oval Office. The June 20, 1972, conversation was misunderstood, he maintained. He valiantly tried to explain away his Watergate role during the Frost interviews and later in his book, reacting angrily when Frost pointed to inconsistencies in his arguments and pressed him for details about his personal involvement. One of the reasons Nixon could do this is that only a few hours of the Watergate tapes had been released by 1994, the year he died. Just as the Nixon administration had carefully kept control over the records, memos, and notes of its staff members, so did the Nixon family and the Nixon Library keep a stranglehold on the Nixon papers and the taped conversations of the February 1971 to July 1973 period. Of course, the Nixon lawyers could not forever escape the persistence of University of Wisconsin law professor Stanley Kutler, and between 1996 and 2002 more than 1,500 hours of the tapes were released for public review. The remaining tapes were to be released later in the first decade of the twenty-first century, opening a window for fresh perspectives on the Nixon years.

After the publication of his book, Nixon began to make public appearances around the United States. His first was in Hyden, Kentucky, in 1978. The conservative populace of the hinterland coal-mining community gave Nixon a warm welcome while he dedicated a recreation center named after him. During the 1980s he made many controlled appearances and found the conservative national trend tended to generate sympathy toward him and his presidency. At the same time, he could issue subtle remarks about the press and what he perceived as its overwhelming influence in Washington. The public received these remarks approvingly during Ronald Reagan's administration, when a critical press did not see eye-to-eye with a Reagan-adoring public. The voters' hostile atmosphere toward the media encouraged such remarks.

To some extent, Nixon's strategy worked. Many had wanted Nixon to succeed during his presidency, if only to quell the chaos in the country. The Watergate scandal was complex, and only the most avid Washington watchers fully understood the implications of what had occurred. To many people, it was still just a lot of politics and they wondered if those who had opposed both

Nixon's decisions involving the Vietnam conflict and his attitudes toward the press were the same ones who drove him from office. While he was president, Main Street was disturbed about his presence in the White House. After his presidency, middle Americans asked themselves just what had he done wrong. Most of the early written history of the Nixon administration after he left office was shrill criticism or sappy support. As has been pointed out, the historical record was woefully inadequate, and so the myth of the Nixon persecution persisted, fanned by the Nixon public relations campaign.

Still, the mood of the country and the public's perception of the role of the president changed for the worse in the 1970s. Economic turmoil contributed to this, but the televised hearings and all the tangential Watergate coverage soured the public on the presidency, if not necessarily on Nixon. Since 1933 and Franklin D. Roosevelt's first years in office, the government and the president were seen as the champions of the people. Now the president was a conniver and the government was filled with paid operatives who spied on innocent private citizens. Nixon himself had said as much. Presidents do the kinds of things that were revealed in the Watergate hearings. That was just the way it was. Until the 1970s, the public was just not fully aware of it, Nixon argued. And in that respect, he was correct. Now they were aware of it.

This theme of presidential malevolence played out in books, movies, and television shows. Government was not a guardian, but a sinister force—one that kept the truth from the public and preyed upon unsuspecting voters. "Before Watergate, presidents were given the benefit of the doubt by the media. After Watergate, they were presumed to be doing the wrong thing until proven otherwise. The burden had shifted. That's a very difficult burden," John Dean observed.[7] Jimmy Carter was able to capitalize on this antigovernment, anti-Washington feeling in 1976 when he defeated Ford by promising to stand up for the little people and not for "government big shots." Carter's shortcomings only convinced the public that the "other kind of president," who could handle the office and stand up for the people, probably did not exist.

The real damage, then, was not the short-term political changes that came to Washington. It was the long-term impact. Election reform flared and then died as politicians placed their personal political careers above the public's need for more effective election financing laws. Other revelations touched off the public distaste for national politics and federal lawmaking. Medical experiments had been performed on prisoners in the 1930s without their knowledge. Unsuspecting soldiers had been exposed to atomic radiation in the 1950s with the knowledge and approval of the military. J. Edgar Hoover had kept dossiers on everyone in Washington during his long tenure as FBI director and had remained in his position by blackmailing everyone, including presidents. John F. Kennedy had cheated on his wife frequently, engaging in lurid and lascivious relationships with beautiful women. Lyndon Johnson had lied about casualty figures, war strategy, government assessments of the war, and all manner of information released during the war in Southeast Asia. All these revelations during the post-Watergate era fanned the fires of mistrust.

Dean blamed the war in Southeast Asia for the malaise more than Watergate. "That had started well before Watergate. Watergate had given it a nudge on down creating distrust, but it really had existed long before Watergate. It was part of a trend," he said.[8]

That somewhat downplays the influence of Watergate, but there is no question that the two historical occurrences, the Vietnam War and the Watergate scandal, coming so close together, had a lasting psychological impact upon Americans. A palpable public mood alteration took place in the immediate post-Watergate years. Presidents were liars. Government was bad. All politicians were alike, because Nixon pointed out that he had done nothing that had not been undertaken by several presidents before him. Naïveté was gone. Cynicism replaced it, and with cynicism came anger. It was not right what had happened, and the voters searched for someone who would make it right. First, Jimmy Carter and then after his failures, Ronald Reagan. The 1970s was a time of turmoil and mistrust, partly because of Nixon and Watergate but also because of the revelations about government. It was a time of disappointment, to be sure.

This helps explain why the public in the 1970s and into the 1980s could not detach itself from the Watergate aftermath. The Teapot Dome scandal during the Warren Harding administration in the early 1920s had hardly caused a ripple. By the time details of the malfeasance reached the public in 1923, Harding had died of a stroke. His successor, Calvin Coolidge, had not been involved in the scandal and Secretary of the Interior Albert Fall was sent to prison for his role, so the average voter was reassured and more interested in finding a bootlegged drink than politics by that time anyway. Teapot Dome was easily understood. Greedy politicians had accepted bribes and an indifferent president had been duped. It was not a tangle of covert activities, wholesale paranoia, and misguided ideology. It was simply a matter of some thieves being caught in the act.

Besides, there was no television in the 1920s. It is ironic that Watergate is seen as a battle between the *Washington Post* and the White House. By the 1970s the print media had become a secondary source of information and a secondary source of concern for the president. The *Washington Post* kept the story alive, but television and the Watergate hearings drove the president from office. John Dean claims that the *Washington Post* and the print media generally had little to do with the uncovering of the Watergate scandal. "The *Washington Post* truly did not crack the case," Dean recalled. "A lot of people have the impression, particularly young people today who have only watched *All the President's Men* on television or perhaps read the book, that this really brought Nixon down. That's not true. The cover-up brought Nixon down of its own weight. They [the press] couldn't have been further from the story as to what was going on. They didn't have anything really on the cover-up at all. ... They had no idea of the width and breadth of the abuse of power that was going on inside the White House." Dean blamed reporters' laziness. They simply went to the White House for chats and expected to get stories. He credited only Bob Woodward and Carl Bernstein, under the direction of editor Ben Bradlee, in breaking that trend, but he still said the *Washington Post* played only a minor role in Watergate.[9] Dean exaggerates to some extent, but by Nixon's time, taming the media, particularly television, was a full-time job and regarded as the most important one in the White House. Nixon alerted the public to the power of television, but his all-out war only alienated a powerful segment of the Washington establishment and confused the public.

Still, the Nixon circle succeeded well enough that once the infatuation with Woodward and Bernstein passed, the public wondered about the role of the press generally in Washington. Many were still convinced that Nixon was right about the excessive power of the media. Many of the movies that depicted the president and government as unscrupulous guardians also placed reporters in the same category. The movie reporter was no longer the crusading Jimmy Stewart character but the unprincipled Sally Fields one (*Absence of Malice*, 1981). Reporters were out only for vengeance and self-aggrandizement. Almost no one and no group in Washington came out of Watergate with a burnished image.

LINGERING POST-WATERGATE ERA

Why did the post-Watergate era continue for so long? Why in the 1990s was there so much public cynicism toward both the press and the presidency? Could it still be that the aftermath of the Nixon administration continued even then? That question requires a brief examination of the presidents who succeeded Nixon and the events of their administrations.

Nixon had promised to bring the nation together. Quite the opposite occurred. A politician making promises and then breaking them is a story as old as the republic, but in the 1970s, television could replay the film of the president making those promises, and a vast complex of media organizations could refresh the public's memory frequently as well. When Jimmy Carter took office, he promised never to tell a lie, a promise he came much closer to keeping than did Nixon with his promise of healing the nation. Yet, Carter could not adequately handle the failing economy, rising unemployment, ruinous inflation, and an international kidnapping in Iran. Few thought of Jimmy Carter as a devious liar, but neither did most of the public see him as a competent national administrator. Carter was the alternative to Watergate and to Washington insiders. He was the outsider free of taint, and his administration proved to be only slightly better than Nixon's.

Additionally, Carter employed a personal friend and public relations person, Jody Powell, as his press secretary. Powell was young and inexperienced; not only did he not appreciate the intricacies of the jobs of the White House correspondents but also he did not try to mend relations that had been tattered first by Watergate and then by the pardon. Instead of reaching out to reporters,

Carter hired media consultants to mold his image and then reacted to press criticism with angry silence. In short, Jimmy Carter was supposed to be everything that Richard Nixon was not, but instead he was everything Nixon had been minus the covert activity. Carter resumed the policies of press manipulation and press antagonism, because he felt abused and unfairly criticized by the press corps generally—a familiar theme that in the late 1970s seemed to transcend political and ideological borders.

With Ronald Reagan's ascendancy to the presidency, press manipulation became a science. The large White House staff spent much of its time monitoring the media and trying to squeeze positive stories from the press corps. Reagan spokespersons Larry Speakes and Marlin Fitzwater were less antagonistic to the correspondents than was Jody Powell, but they were only small parts of a huge press apparatus designed to obfuscate rather than to inform. When, in late 1986, it was revealed that arms had been traded with Iran, a violation of Reagan's own policies, and then sent to the Contras in Nicaragua, it was clear that covert activities had not died with the Nixon resignation. Reagan denied any knowledge of the secret arms deal, even when an independent prosecutor claimed seven years later that both he and Vice President George H. W. Bush knew of the illegal activities. Though the public generally forgave Reagan at the end of his years in office, it was clear that the presidency had once again been damaged.

Clearly, then, two things had developed by the late 1980s: the public had been reminded continually that presidents were really just politicians elevated to more elegant surroundings, and the press office had become nothing more than a clearinghouse for public relations initiatives. The answer to the question of why Watergate lingered for so many years was that each succeeding president—through attempted press manipulation, poor administrative judgment, or tolerance of illicit activities under their jurisdictions—had reminded both the press and the public what Watergate had represented. Each time the memories of Watergate began to fade, they were revived. The post-Watergate cynicism of the 1970s was institutionalized by the end of the 1980s after the Iran-Contra scandal. Raw cynicism washed from Main Street over the banks of the Potomac and into the halls of government. Reporters looked for the kind of negative images that the public expected and fanned the cynicism. They also personalized the presidency, looking not only for weaknesses in policies and programs, but also for foibles in the president's personal life. People forgot what Watergate was about, but they did not lose the cynicism that it generated.

Not all changes in Washington can be attached directly to post-Watergate skepticism, but there is more connection in many cases than one might see at first glance. By the late 1980s, public disenchantment with the national political process had gone beyond anger and sinking realization. It had reached a point of indifference. In 1996, voter participation in the presidential election dropped to 49 percent, the lowest rate in American history. Interest in issue-oriented Washington news dipped perceptibly.

Beginning with stories about Democratic presidential candidate Gary Hart's personal relationship with model Donna Rice in 1987, journalists concentrated on the foibles of presidents and presidential candidates, topics that previously had been taboo for mainstream media reporters. A national reporter who worked for a major mainstream newspaper told the author that the newspaper had asked her in 2000 to spend a whole year delving into George W. Bush's early personal life, chasing down one rumor after another. In a conversation with Bush, who refused to comment on such matters, the reporter said: "The public has a right to know about the president's personal life."

Why would a respected reporter for a major, influential newspaper in the twenty-first century say such a thing? One reason was that the media had changed. Interest in issue-oriented news had dwindled, and bureau staffs for the networks, for the national newsmagazines, and for major newspapers had been cut in the late 1980s. This was in part because of corporate mergers and leveraged buyouts of media organizations, which resulted in more emphasis on the bottom line and less concern for the role of the journalist in keeping an eye on government, but it also had to do with the public's tepid demand to know what was happening with their tax dollars in Washington. Readers and viewers hardly cared.

George H. W. Bush tried valiantly to deal with reporters fully and fairly with long and frequent press conferences during which he answered correspondents' questions fully. Reporters liked Bush personally, but that did not translate to positive press coverage. Because of a slight downturn in the economy in 1991, Bush was described daily as a failure. He was defeated in office in a spirited three-way campaign in 1992 that brought Arkansas Governor William Jefferson Clinton to office. With the Clinton administration came the most absurd reporting trend in modern times. Reporters struggled to cover issues, but they enthusiastically explored the lascivious relationships that Clinton undertook—and there were many. Public skepticism had bred indifference, which spawned a concentration on salacious storytelling. Clinton provided all the fodder that any Hollywood gossip columnist, let alone a Washington correspondent, might seek.

By the time George W. Bush took office in 2001, reporters had trouble even recognizing an issue worthy of their concern until the national calamity of September 11, 2001, when minions of terrorist Osama bin Laden crashed two jets into New York's World Trade Center twin towers and a third into the Pentagon in Washington. Only when more than 3,000 persons died in a calamity that destroyed billions of dollars worth of property did Americans become energized about their country and the issues that plagued it.

Meanwhile, the role of the presidential press secretary continued to deteriorate in the waning years of the twentieth century. That is not to say that press secretaries failed to generate reasonable relationships with reporters on occasion. Fitzwater continued as the senior Bush's press secretary after Reagan left office, and Clinton's stable of four press secretaries was highlighted by a credible job performed by his second press officer, Michael McCurry. Still, the office of press secretary itself dwindled in importance. It became part of a vast press apparatus centered on public opinion polls and spin control. "You know, I don't remember that the term *spin control* was ever used when I covered the White House," Jerry Landay remembered. "That kind of thing happened with Nixon, but we just wouldn't have used a term like that or consciously accepted being manipulated in such a way."[10]

Eventually, the media stopped referring to the president's press officer as a "press secretary" and stories about the White House simply referred to the press liaison as "a presidential spokesperson." There was no attempt to pretend that the office was there to help reporters, only to manipulate them. The mutual suspicion between reporters and the White House staff became institutionalized. The press secretary no longer served two masters.

MEANING OF THE NIXON YEARS

"Toward the end, I really wanted to just go away and rest. I was terribly depressed," Landay recalled as he discussed the final months of the Nixon administration. "I was depressed by the amount of chicanery in the White House ... and I was depressed about what had become of the Office of the President of the United States. I remember when we were in California during those last weeks [of Nixon's term of office], I pulled Alexander Haig aside and asked him, 'Why do you keep doing this? Why do you stick around?' And he answered, 'Because of the Office of the President. It needs to be protected.' He made a point of the distinction between Nixon and the Office of the Presidency. I think that's important."[11]

What, then, was the meaning of the Nixon presidency to the Office of the Presidency and to the press-president-public interrelationship? Obviously, Nixon and his cohorts embarrassed the nation, and the presidency suffered for it. But each president who followed Nixon had the opportunity to return some prestige to the highest political office in the land. What each did instead was develop more sophisticated ways to control the press, especially television (with the exception of George H. W. Bush), but failed to do so. Reporters and media organizations had the options to return journalism to worthier paths and to restore public faith in their efforts to protect the interests of the nation. Their collective decisions to do otherwise cannot be blamed wholly on Richard Nixon or Watergate. Yet, as has been documented here, the aftermath of the Nixon administration did not die easily, and the twin by-products of mistrust and apathy began with revelations from the Watergate hearings and the Watergate tapes. Despite Nixon's best efforts, informed Americans know exactly what Nixon planned, how he planned it, and what he sought to gain from White House covert activities.

In historical retrospect, Richard Nixon may not have been responsible for all the mistrust and shoddy activities that followed his presidency, but he and his inner circle certainly started the nation in that direction. We know now from the evidence that, despite all the explanations and justifications that were offered later, Nixon oversaw one of the most corrupt and immoral administrations in U.S. history, and we know that an abnormal preoccupation with the influence of the press was largely responsible for the most despicable of White House covert activities. We also know that the country has had great difficulty in reclaiming the moral high ground that was lost during Watergate. Even into the twenty-first century the effects of Vietnam and Watergate linger just beneath the surface.

NOTES

1. "Remarks at the Annual Dinner of the White House Correspondents Association," in *Public Papers of the President: Richard Nixon 1973* (Washington: Government Printing Office, 1973), 288.

2. John Dean, telephone interview with author, January 15, 2002.

3. Jerry Landay, interview with author, December 20, 2001.

4. John F. Kennedy Library and Foundation Newsletter (online) at www.jfklibrary .org/newsletter summer2001_01.html.

5. John Dean, telephone interview with author, January 15, 2002.

6. Thomas J. Johnson, *The Rehabilitation of Richard Nixon: The Media's Effect on Collective Memory* (New York: Garland, 1995), 14.

7. John Dean, telephone interview with author, January 15, 2002.

8. Ibid.

9. Ibid.

10. Jerry Landay, interview with author, December 20, 2001.

11. Ibid.

Appendix A

Cast of Nixon Characters

Richard M. Nixon, president, January 20, 1969, to August 9, 1974

Spiro Agnew, vice president, resigned October 10, 1973

Gerald R. Ford, vice president, December 6, 1973, to August 8, 1974; president August 9, 1974, to January 20, 1977

Harry Robbins (Bob) Haldeman, chief of staff, resigned April 30, 1973

John Ehrlichman, chief advisor for domestic affairs, resigned April 30, 1973

Patrick Buchanan, speechwriter and presidential aide

Herbert Klein, director of communications (succeeded in June 1973 by Kenneth Clawson)

Ronald Ziegler, press secretary

Diane Sawyer, Ziegler aide

Dwight Chapin, Nixon appointments secretary

Alexander Butterfield, presidential aide who revealed the existence of the taping system during Senate Watergate Committee testimony in July 1973

Charles Colson, presidential aide (chief hatchet man)

John Dean, counsel to the president (in charge of the cover-up); revealed the cover-up during June 25, 1973, testimony before the Watergate Committee; author of the statement to Nixon on March 21, 1972: "There is a cancer on the presidency." Resigned April 30, 1973

Rose Mary Woods, Nixon's secretary; forced to claim she accidentally erased 18½ minutes of the June 20, 1972, conversation between Nixon and Haldeman

Daniel Ellsberg, national security advisor under Lyndon Johnson who leaked the Pentagon Papers to the press in 1971

Lewis Fielding, Ellsberg's psychiatrist; his office in Beverly Hills was burglarized in September 1971 by the "plumbers," who were trying to get negative information about Ellsberg

Ben Bradlee, executive editor of *Washington Post*; in charge of the Watergate investigation

Carl Bernstein and *Bob Woodward, Post* reporters who uncovered the Watergate scandal and helped the *Post* win two Pulitzer Prizes

Katherine Graham, Washington Post publisher

Alexander Haig, Haldeman's successor; some believe he was Deep Throat; later was Reagan's secretary of state

E. Howard Hunt and *G. Gordon Liddy,* Watergate burglary organizers; former CIA agent Hunt received $10,000 in hush money; Liddy was a former FBI agent

James McCord (formerly of the CIA) and four Cuban expatriates, burglars at the Watergate

Donald Segretti, in charge of dirty tricks during the 1972 campaign

Herbert Kalmbach, Nixon lawyer and aide who provided funding for Segretti's dirty tricks from an illegal campaign fund

John J. Sirica, U.S. district judge, oversaw the Watergate grand jury investigation

John Mitchell, attorney general and then director of the Committee to Re-Elect the President (CREEP) in 1972

Sam Ervin, Democratic senator from North Carolina, chair of the Watergate Committee

Archibald Cox, special prosecutor from May to October 1972 (fired in the Saturday Night Massacre)

Leon Jaworski, special prosecutor from October 1972 to 1974

Elliot Richardson, defense secretary and then in 1972 attorney general until his resignation under pressure on October 20, 1973 (Saturday Night Massacre)

William Ruckelshaus, deputy attorney general, fired October 20, 1973

Robert Bork, solicitor general, fired Cox after Richardson and Ruckelshaus refused to

Edmund Muskie, senator from Maine, Democratic front-runner in 1972 primaries; victim of dirty tricks; discredited after tearful speech in front of *Manchester Union-Leader* (February 1972); withdrew soon afterward

Edward Kennedy, Massachusetts Democratic senator, not a candidate in 1972 because of accident at Chappaquiddick

George McGovern, South Dakota senator, Nixon's Democratic opponent in 1972

George Wallace, Democratic Alabama governor, shot by Arthur Bremer while campaigning in May 1972 (wheelchair user thereafter)

Hubert Humphrey, Lyndon Johnson's vice president and Democratic nominee in 1968; beaten by McGovern in 1972 primaries

J. Edgar Hoover, longtime director of the FBI who died in May 1972, kept dossiers on officials in Washington for blackmail

L. Patrick Gray, succeeded Hoover; refused to bow to White House pressure to cover up Watergate; was not confirmed by Senate in spring 1973

Nixon Administration Timeline

November 5, 1968	Nixon barely defeats Humphrey for the presidency
Spring 1969	Operatives begin bugging homes and offices of Nixon's opponents, journalists
November 3, 1969	Agnew, speaking in Des Moines, Iowa, attacks news media
April 30, 1970	Nixon TV speech reveals Cambodia secret bombing
May 4, 1970	Kent State University shootings
February 1971 to July 1973	Secret audiotaping of conversations in Oval Office, in Executive Office, on White House phones, and at Camp David
February 23, 1971	CBS documentary "Selling of the Pentagon" airs
June 13, 1971	Pentagon Papers begin appearing in the *New York Times* and then the *Washington Post* (leaked by former National Security Advisor Daniel Ellsberg); prior restraint ordered by Supreme Court; publication resumes three weeks later after ruling favors press
June 1971	Watergate "plumbers" unit formed and housed in the basement of the White House
September 1971	Plumbers break into offices of Ellsberg psychiatrist Lewis Fielding, Beverly Hills
Fall 1971	Donald Segretti begins dirty tricks against Democratic presidential candidates
February 1972	Tearful Muskie speech at *Manchester* (N.H.) *Union-Leader*

February 1972	Nixon visit to China
June 1972	McGovern wraps up Democratic nomination with primary wins
June 17, 1972	Break-in at Democratic National Headquarters in the Watergate hotel-office-apartment complex; burglars arrested; Woodward and Bernstein begin investigation
June 20, 1972	Watergate cover-up begins, Nixon-Haldeman conversation takes place, is later erased
June 23, 1972	First of "smoking gun" conversations
June 30, 1972	Mitchell resigns as head of CREEP for "personal reasons"
August 1972	Raucous convention hurts McGovern; Missouri Senator Thomas Eagleton named to ticket; Eagleton resigns weeks later in favor of Sargent Shriver, former Peace Corps director and Kennedy in-law
September 15, 1972	Second "smoking gun" conversation; on same day, Hunt, Liddy, and five burglars are indicted
November 7, 1972	Nixon handily defeats McGovern
January 1973	U.S.-Hanoi pact signed; U.S. participation in Vietnam ends
March 1973	Facing prison, McCord writes to federal District Judge John Sirica telling him he knows much more but has been ordered to keep quiet; he testifies again
March, 21, 1973	Nixon-Dean "cancer on presidency" "smoking gun" talk
April 30, 1973	Ehrlichman, Haldeman, Kleindeinst, and Dean resign; Haig and Kissinger (now secretary of state) become key Nixon advisors
May 1973	Testimony before Senate Watergate Committee begins
June 6, 1973	Klein quits; communication chores given to Ziegler
June 25, 1973	Dean tells committee about the cover-up and the "cancer on the presidency" discussion that took place March 21, 1973
July 13, 1973	Butterfield reveals existence of tapes to investigators, testifies three days later
August 29, 1973	Sirica rules that Nixon must hand over tapes; ruling upheld by Appeals Court on October 12
October 10, 1973	Agnew pleads nolo contendere in 1966 income tax case and resigns

October 20, 1973	Richardson resigns; Ruckelshaus is fired by Haldeman; Bork fires Cox
November 1, 1973	Jaworski replaces Cox; Judiciary Committee considers impeachment hearings
November 15, 1973	Nixon turns over a few of the tapes, reveals 18½-minute gap on June 20, 1972, tape
December 6, 1973	House confirms Ford as new vice president after Senate confirmation on November 26, 1973
February 21, 1974	Impeachment report given to House Judiciary Committee
July 24, 1974	U.S. Supreme Court rules, 8–0, that Nixon must release all pertinent tapes
July 27–29, 1974	Three impeachment articles are passed, sent to full House
August 5, 1974	Nixon releases tapes, including "smoking gun" tape of June 23, 1974, in which he directs the cover-up
August 8, 1974	After many in GOP abandon Nixon, he announces in a national television address that he will resign at noon the next day
August 9, 1974	Nixon resigns, flies to San Clemente; Ford is sworn in
September 8, 1974	Ford announces Nixon pardon; press secretary Jerald terHorst resigns, is replaced by NBC correspondent Ronald Nessen
1973–1975	Twenty-five Watergate figures are imprisoned, including Mitchell, Haldeman, Ehrlichman, Dean, Colson, Segretti, Hunt, Liddy, and the five burglars

Appendix C

Major Newspaper Coverage of Watergate
June 17–December 31, 1972

	Staff news stories	Wire service news stories (AP, UPI)	Washington Post, LA Times, New York Times or other Syndicate stories	Editorials	Columns/Opinion
New York Times	99	6	1	10	2
Washington Post	201	4	0	17	14
St. Louis Post-Dispatch	12	45	13	8	1
Rocky Mountain News	15	74	0	4	13
Chicago Tribune	30	13	7	1	9
Chicago Sun-Times	21	27	36	5	2
Wall Street Journal	18	0	0	0	0
Atlanta Journal & Constitution	2	39	16	2	11
San Francisco Chronicle	2	50	55	0	3
Los Angeles Times	45	44	32	13	2
Christian Science Monitor	26	9	2	6	5
New Orleans Times-Picayune	1	21	0	0	1
Detroit Free Press	25	46	6	6	27
Minneapolis Tribune	12	25	36	4	4
Houston Post	7	2	35	0	14

Selected Bibliography

BOOKS

Ambrose, Stephen. *Nixon: The Education of a Politician*. New York: Simon & Schuster, 1987.

——. *Nixon: Volume Two—The Triumph of a Politician, 1962–1972*. New York: Simon & Schuster, 1989.

Anderson, Jack, and James Boyd. *Confessions of a Muckraker*. New York: Random House, 1979.

Baughman, James L. *The Republic of Mass Culture: Journalism, Filmmaking, and Broadcasting in America since 1941*. Baltimore: Johns Hopkins, 1992.

Ben-Veniste, Richard. *Stonewall: The Real Story of the Watergate Prosecution*. New York: Simon & Schuster, 1977.

Berry, Joseph P. *John F. Kennedy and the Media: The First Television President*. Lanham, Md.: University Press of America, 1987.

Bochin, Hal W. *Richard Nixon: Rhetorical Strategist*. Westport, Conn.: Greenwood, 1990.

Brodie, Fawn. *Richard Nixon: The Shaping of His Character*. New York W. W. Norton, 1981.

Burke, Vincent J., and Vee Burke. *Nixon's Good Deed: Welfare Reform*. New York: Columbia University Press, 1992.

Calvocoressi, Peter. *World Politics since 1945*. London: Longman, 1982.

Cantril, Albert H., ed. *Polling on the Issues: Twenty-One Perspectives on the Role of Opinion Polls in the Making of Public Policy*. Washington: Seven Locks Press, 1963.

Cohen, Bernard C. *The Press and Foreign Policy*. Princeton, N.J.: Princeton University Press, 1963.

Colodny, Len. *Silent Coup: The Removal of a President*. New York: St. Martin's Press, 1992.

Colson, Charles W. *Born Again*. Old Tappan, N.J.: Chosen Books, 1976.

Cornwell, Elmer E. *Presidential Leadership of Public Opinion*. Bloomington: Indiana University Press, 1956.

Cronin, Thomas E. *The State of the Presidency*. Boston: Little Brown, 1975.

Crouse, Timothy. *The Boys on the Bus: Riding with the Campaign Press Corps*. New York: Random House, 1973.

Crowley, Monica. *Nixon in Winter*. New York: Random House, 1998.

Deakin, James. *Straight Stuff: The Reporters, the White House, and the Truth*. New York: William Morrow, 1984.

Dean, John. *Blind Ambition: The White House Years*. New York: Simon & Schuster, 1976.

———. *Lost Honor*. Los Angeles: Stratford Press, 1982.

———. *The Rehnquist Choice: The Untold Story of the Nixon Appointment That Redefined the Supreme Court*. New York: Free Press, 2001.

Desmond, Robert W. *The Press and World Affairs*. New York: Arno, 1972.

Dickerson, Nancy. *Among Those Present: A Reporter's Viewpoint of Twenty-Five Years in Washington*. New York: Random House, 1976.

Dinsmore, Herman H. *All the News That Fits: A Critical Analysis of the News and Editorial Content of the New York Times*. New Rochelle, N.Y.: Arlington House, 1969.

Donovan, Hedley. *Roosevelt to Reagan: A Reporter's Encounters with Nine Presidents*. New York: Harper & Row, 1985.

Dover, E.D. *Presidential Elections in the Television Age*. Westport, Conn.: Praeger, 1994.

Drew, Elizabeth. *Washington Journal: The Events of 1973–1974*. New York: Random House, 1975.

Edwards, George. *The Public Presidency*. New York: St. Martin's, 1983.

Ehrlichman, John. *Witness to Power: The Nixon Years*. New York: Simon & Schuster, 1982.

Eisenhower, Julie Nixon. *Pat Nixon: The Untold Story*. New York: Simon & Schuster, 1986.

Emery, Edwin, and Michael Emery *The Press and America: An Interpretive History of the Mass Media*. 5th ed. Englewood Cliffs, N.J.: Prentice-Hall, 1984.

Emery, Fred. *Watergate: The Corruption of American Politics and the Fall of Richard Nixon*. New York: Times Books, 1994.

Ervin, Sam J. *The Whole Truth: Watergate by Sam Ervin*. New York: Random House, 1980.

Friedman, Leon, and William F. Levantrosser eds. *Watergate and Afterward: The Legacy of Richard M. Nixon*. Westport, Conn.: Greenwood Press, 1992.

Frost, David. *"I Gave Them a Sword": Behind the Scenes of the Nixon Interviews*. New York: Morrow, 1978.

Gallup, George H. *The Gallup Poll: Public Opinion 1935–1971*, Vol. 1. New York: Random House, 1972.

Garment, Leonard. *In Search of Deep Throat: The Greatest Political Mystery of Our Time*. New York: Basic Books, 2000.

Garthoff, Raymond L. *Detente and Confrontation: American-Soviet Relations from Nixon to Reagan*. Washington, D.C.: Brookings Institute, 1985.

Garza, Hedda. *The Watergate Investigation Index: House Judiciary Hearings and Report on Impeachment*. Wilmington, Del.: Scholarly Resources, 1985.

————. *The Watergate Investigation Index: Senate Select Committee Hearings and Reports on Presidential Campaign Activities.* Wilmington, Del.: Scholarly Resources, 1982.

Gelman, Harry. *The Brezhnev Politburo and the Decline of Detente.* Ithaca, N.Y.: Cornell University Press, 1984.

Genovese, Michael A. *The Watergate Crisis.* Westport, Conn.: Greenwood, 1999.

Graber, Doris. *Mass Media and American Politics,* 2nd ed. Washington, DC: CQ Press, 1984.

Gutline, Myra. *The President's Partner: The First Lady of the Twentieth Century.* New York: Greenwood, 1989.

Haig, Alexander M., Jr. *Inner Circles: How America Changed the World.* New York: Warner, 1992.

Halberstam, David. *The Best and the Brightest.* Greenwich, Conn.: Fawcett, 1973.

————. *The Powers That Be.* New York: Alfred A. Knopf, 1979.

Haldeman, H. R. *The Ends of Power.* New York: New York Times Books, 1978.

————. *The Haldeman Diaries: Inside the Nixon White House.* New York: G. P. Putnam's Sons, 1994.

Herring, George C. *America's Longest War: The United States and Vietnam 1950–1975,* 2nd ed. New York: Alfred A. Knopf, 1986.

Hersh, Seymour M. *The Price of Power: Kissinger in the Nixon White House.* New York: Summit, 1983.

Hoff, Joan. *Watergate Revisited.* Greenville, N.C.: East Carolina University Press, 1993.

Hoffman, Paul. *The New Nixon.* New York: Tower, 1970.

Isaacs, Arthur R. *Without Honor: Defeat in Vietnam and Cambodia.* New York: Vintage, 1982.

Isaacson, Walter. *Henry Kissinger: A Biography.* New York: Simon & Schuster, 1992.

Jamieson, Kathleen Hall. *Packaging the Presidency: A History of Criticism of Presidential Campaign Activity.* New York: Oxford University Press, 1984.

Jaworski, Leon. *The Right and the Power: The Prosecution of Watergate.* New York: Reader's Digest Press, 1976.

Johnson, George W., ed. *The Nixon Presidential Press Conferences.* New York: Earl Coleman, 1978.

Johnson, Richard Tanner. *Managing the White House: An Intimate Study of the Presidency.* New York: Harper & Row, 1974.

Keogh, James. *President Nixon and the Press.* New York: Funk & Wagnalls, 1972.

————. *White House Years.* Boston: Little, Brown, 1978.

Kissinger, Henry. *White House Years.* Boston: Little, Brown, 1979.

Klein, Herbert G. *Making It Perfectly Clear.* Garden City, N.Y.: Doubleday, 1980.

Kluger, Richard. *The Paper: The Life and Death of the New York Herald Tribune.* New York: Knopf, 1986.

Kutler, Stanley. *Abuse of Power: The New Nixon Tapes.* New York: The Free Press, 1997.

————. *The Wars of Watergate: The Last Crisis of Richard Nixon.* New York: Alfred A. Knopf, 1990.

Landau, David. *Kissinger: The Uses of Power.* Boston: Houghton Mifflin, 1972.

Lang, Gladys Engel, and Kurt Lang. *The Battle for Public Opinion: The President, the Press, and the Polls during Watergate.* New York: Columbia University, 1983.

Lasky, Victor. *It Didn't Start with Watergate.* New York: Dial, 1977.

Leuchtenburg, William. *In the Shadow of FDR: From Harry Truman to Ronald Reagan.* Ithaca, N.Y.: Cornell University Press, 1983.

Liebovich, Louis W. *The Press and the Modern Presidency: Myths and Mindsets from Kennedy to Election 2000,* 2nd ed. Westport, Conn.: Praeger, 2001.

Light, Paul C. *The President's Agenda: Domestic Policy Choice from Kennedy to Carter.* Baltimore: Johns Hopkins University Press, 1982.

Lukas, J. Anthony. *Nightmare: The Underside of the Nixon Years.* New York: Viking Press, 1976.

Lurie, Leonard. *The Running of Richard Nixon.* New York: Coward, McCann & Geoghegan, 1972.

Magruder, Jeb Stuart. *An American Life: One Man's Road to Watergate.* New York: Atheneum, 1974.

Mankiewicz, Frank. *Perfectly Clear: Nixon from Whittier to Watergate.* New York: Quadrangle, 1973.

McGinniss, Joe. *The Selling of the President 1968.* New York: Trident, 1969.

Mee, Charles. *A Visit to Haldeman and Other States of Mind.* New York: M. Evan, 1977.

Miller, Marvin. *The Breaking of the President: The Nixon Connection.* Covine, Calif.: Classic Publications, 1976.

Moyers, Bill D. *The Secret Government: The Constitution in Crisis.* Lanham, Md.: Seven Locks Press, 1988.

Murray, Robert K., and Tim H. Blessing. *Greatness in the White House: Rating the Presidents,* 2nd ed. University Park: Pennsylvania State University Press, 1994.

Nixon, Richard M. *From the President: Richard Nixon's Secret Files.* New York: Harper & Row, 1988.

———. *RN: The Memoirs of Richard Nixon.* New York: Grosset & Dunlap, 1978.

Olmsted, Kathryn. *Challenging the Secret Government: The Post-Watergate Investigations of the CIA and the FBI.* Chapel Hill: University of North Carolina Press, 1996.

Peterson, Mark A. *Legislating Together: The White House and Capitol Hill from Eisenhower to Reagan.* Cambridge, Mass.: Harvard University Press, 1990.

Polls and Scandals from Nixon to Clinton: A Resource for Journalists. Arlington, Va.: American Association for Public Opinion Research, 1998.

Porter, William E. *Assault on the Media: The Nixon Years.* Ann Arbor: University of Michigan, 1976.

Price, Raymond. *With Nixon.* New York: Viking Press, 1977.

Quandt, William B. *Decade of Decisions: American Policy toward the Arab-Israeli Conflict, 1967–1976.* Berkeley: University of California Press. 1977.

Rather, Dan, and Gary Paul Gates. *The Palace Guard.* New York: Harper & Row, 1974.

Reasoner, Harry. *Before the Colors Fade.* New York: Alfred A. Knopf, 1981.

Reston, James B. *Deadline: A Memoir.* New York: Random House, 1991.

Rivers, William L. *The Other Government: Power and the Washington Media.* New York: Universe Books, 1982.

Safire, William. *Before the Fall.* Garden City, N.Y.: Doubleday, 1975.

Schorr, Daniel. *Clearing the Air.* New York: Berkley, 1978.

Schudson, Michael. *Watergate in American Memory: How We Remember, Forget, and Reconstruct the Past.* New York: Basic Books, 1992.

Sidey, Hugh, and Fred Ward. *Portrait of a President.* New York: Harper & Row, 1975.

Simon, William E. *A Time for Truth.* New York: Berkley, 1978.

Sirica, John J. *To Set the Record Straight: The Break-in, the Tapes, the Conspirators, the Pardon.* New York:

Smith, Hedrick. *The Power Game: How Washington Works.* New York: Random House, 1988.

Sorenson, Theodore. *Watchmen in the Night: Presidential Accountability after Watergate.* Cambridge, Mass.: MIT Press, 1975.

Spalding, Henry D. *The Nixon Nobody Knows.* New York: Jonathan David, 1972.

Spear, Joseph C. *Presidents and the Press: The Nixon Legacy.* Cambridge, Mass.: MIT Press, 1984.

Spragens, William C. *The Presidency and the Mass Media in the Age of Television.* Lanham, Md.: University Press of America, 1979.

Spragens, William C., and Carole Ann Terwoord. *From Spokesperson to Press Secretary: White House Media Operations.* Washington, D.C.: University Press of America, 1980.

Stans, Maurice H. *The Terrors of Justice.* New York: Everest House, 1978.

Sussman, Barry. *The Great Cover-Up: Nixon and the Scandal of Watergate.* New York: Signet, 1974.

Tebell, John, and Sarah Miles Watts. *The Press and the Presidency: From George Washington to Ronald Reagan.* New York: Oxford, 1985.

Weaver, David, Doris Graber, Maxwell McCombs, and Chaim Eyal. *Media Agenda Setting in Presidential Elections.* New York: Praeger, 1981.

Wendt, Lloyd. *Chicago Tribune: The Rise of a Great American Newspaper.* Chicago: Rand McNally, 1979.

White, Theodore. *America in Search of Itself: The Making of the President, 1956–1980.* New York: Harper & Row, 1982.

———. *Breach of Faith: The Fall of Richard Nixon.* New York: Atheneum, 1975.

———. *The Making of the President 1968.* New York: Atheneum, 1969.

———. *The Making of the President 1972.* New York: Atheneum, 1973.

Wicker, Tom. *On Press.* New York: Viking, 1978.

Wills, Gary. *Nixon Agonistes: The Crisis of the Self-Made Man.* New York: New American Library, 1979.

Wilson, Will. *A Fool for a Client.* Austin, Tex.: Eakin Press, 2000.

Witcover, Jules. *The Reconstruction of Richard Nixon.* New York: G. P. Putnam's Sons, 1970.

Woodstone, Arthur. *Nixon's Head.* New York: St. Martin's Press, 1972.

Woodward, Bob. *Shadow: Five Presidents and the Legacy of Watergate.* New York: Simon & Schuster, 1999.

Woodward, Bob, and Carl Bernstein. *All the President's Men.* New York: Simon & Schuster, 1974.

———. *The Final Days.* New York: Simon & Schuster, 1976.

INTERVIEWS

Dean, John. Telephone interview by author, January 15, 2002.
Landay, Jerry. Interview by author, December 20, 2001.

Index

About the Author

LOUIS W. LIEBOVICH is a Professor of Journalism at the University of Illinois, Champaign-Urbana. Professor Liebovich has also written *The Press and the Modern Presidency: Myths and Mindsets from Kennedy to Election 2000*, *The Press and the Origins of the Cold War, 1944–1947*, and *Bylines of Despair: Herbert Hoover, the Great Depression, and the U.S. News Media*, published by Praeger.